The
Souls
of
Your
Feet

"It should now be clear to everyone that this artform is so deep it takes a lifetime to master and yet we're still not finished inventing it!"

Brenda Bufalino

The Souls
of Your Feet

A Tap Dance Guidebook for Rhythm Explorers

by **Acia Gray**

Grand Weaver's Publishing
Austin, TX 1998

Cover design by Acia Gray with Paul Alvarado-Dykstra
Cover artwork by C&M Press, Denver, Colorado
Cover photo by Carol Felauer
Chapter heading photos by Carol Felauer and Elizabeth Cruger
Photo dancers: Nicholas Young, Acia Gray, John Kirkilis,
Karen Honcik and "Smokey" Rhodes.

Editing by Silver Phoenix Literary Services, Austin, TX
Additional editing: Paul Alvarado-Dykstra, Brenda Bufalino,
Lynn Dally and Dianne Walker.
Indexing by Linda Webster

Printing by C&M Press, Denver, Colorado

ISBN 0-9667445-0-0
0 9 8 7 6 5 4

Library of Congress catalog card number 98-87956

Grand Weaver's Publishing
P.O. Box 152995
Austin, TX 78715-2995
512/443-3022
FAX 512/474-9812

SoulsFeet@aol.com
http://members.aol.com/soulsfeet/SoulsFeetWebsite.html

Dedication

To all of the tap dancers in the world beyond.
May your souls be improvising in a heaven of great musicians.

Contents

About the Author

Acia Gray has toured extensively as soloist, choreographer and teacher in over 250 cities across the U.S. and abroad and, along with Deirdre Strand, is the cofounder and Artistic Director of Tapestry Dance Company in Austin, TX, one of the few professional, multiform companies in the country. With TDC, her works have shared the stage with such companies as the New York City Ballet, the Houston Ballet and Doug Varone & Dancers among many others.

After graduating from the American Academy of Dramatic Arts, NYC, Ms. Gray began her professional dance career as a principal dancer and Managing Director of Austin on Tap, one of the busiest touring tap companies in the 1980's. As a soloist, she has since shared the stage with such tap greats as Steve Condos, Jimmy Slyde, Lon Chaney, Chuck Green, Sarah Petronio, Brenda Bufalino, Dianne Walker, Sam Weber and Savion Glover among many others.

Ms. Gray was chosen as one of 12 dancers worldwide to work with tap legend Charles "Honi" Coles in America's first Creative Residency in the art of tap at the Colorado Dance Festival and again in 1990 with Jimmy Slyde. She has appeared in *The Great Tap Reunion, Tap/Dowop, Chicago on Tap,* the Las Vegas *Tribute to Cholly Atkins, Just Friends* with Sarah Petronio and the PBS documentary *Honi Coles — A Class Act.*

Ms. Gray is an original steering committee member of the International Tap Association and has taught for the New York City Tap Festival, the Chicago Human Rhythm Project, the Southeastern Tap Explosion, the International Summer School/Cyprus, Dance Masters of

America, the Dance Center of Columbia College, the Colorado Dance Festival, Chicago on Tap, the University of Texas, the Texas Association Teachers of Dance and numerous other college, theatre, community dance organizations and tap festivals.

In addition to Tapestry works, her choreography has been commissioned by Ballet Austin, St. Louis' Tapsichore, numerous modern dance choreographers and equity productions of *She Loves Me, Cabaret, My Fair Lady, Man of La Mancha* and *Nunsense!* among others. Ms. Gray continues as choreographer, collaborator, educator and dancer in the effort to bridge the gap between traditional and contemporary views of dance and American rhythm tap.

". . . makes tap look like pure joy."
Chicago Sun—Times

"(a) tapping tornado - funny, sexy and real."
the Village Voice

"(she) looks inside herself, not to find a stage persona, but to give the most responsive, personal performance possible."
Dance Magazine

"her dancing keeps us riveted . . ."
Washington Dance Review

Acknowledgments

ALL MY LOVE AND THANKS TO: the late Charles "Honi" Coles for changing my life and turning me inside out; my dearest friend Sarah Petronio who teaches me constantly what's really important and truly knows how to sing with her feet; Brenda Bufalino for her guidance over the years, the American Tap Dance Orchestra and those sharing moments in Chicago; Debra Bray who laid the footwork foundation for my future; the late Steve Condos for his rudiments and Louis Armstrong stories; Marda Kirn and the 1989 Colorado Dance Festival; Ethel Siegel & Siegel Artist Management for their love and support in my career; Dianne Walker for her incredible rhythmic voice, her stories and her wonderful "flash" steps; Lynn Dally for her constant strive for tap dance as an artform through the Jazz Tap Ensemble; Camden Richman for unknowingly being my idol for many years; the late Chuck Green for this delicate, big feet and quiet stories; the late Lon Chaney for our last performance together — it was an honor; Jimmy Slyde for saying "Don't do everything you know!" and then sharing everything he does; Jan Feager for being a true friend in this crazy world of rhythm; Nicholas Young for showing me that we are truly part of a legacy; Sam Weber for those incredible legs; Katherine Kramer for her historical research and comic timing; Leela Petronio for *Moanin'* and continuing to share her soul through tap; Fred Moritel for Eddie's B.S. Chorus and a year of fun; Sam Katz for keeping me connected to California; Mark Mendonca for being one of the nicest guys I've ever danced with; Savion Glover for pushing the limits of tap dance and for that wonderful duet with his Mom in St. Louis; Yvette Glover for her smile and her undying faith in our tap family; Gregory Hines for his continuing promotion of tap dance, taking the time in NYC and the free class for my students;

Anita Feldman for those incredible polyrhythmic master classes many years ago and sharing her craft through *Inside Tap*; Rusty Frank for getting her wonderful book *Tap!* on every bookshelf in America; Sandman Sims for being my first "hoofer"; the late Eddie Brown's *Scientific Rhythm* and "Can you dig it?"; Melba Huber for helping to keep tap alive and sharing it with the world through her writing; Cholly Atkins for his "groovin" classes and contributions to Motown and the legacy of tap; pianist Bross Townsend for greatly influencing my improvisational voice; Rich Harney for his musical genius and continuing to be an inspiration; A.D. Mannion for being one of the best drummers in the universe; all of my students over the years who have taught me what dance is all about; the current and past members of Tapestry Dance Company who challenge my creative muse; Cindy Brittain and John Reicker for their incredible friendship and soul connection; my Mom and Dad who bought me that first set of drums; and to Deirdre Strand who put me back on that stage and shares my life of. . .

soul searching.

Foreword

Through the years of living my life as a dancer, I have often pondered the question of why? Why am I? Why have I created a life for myself as a tap dancer? Living such a legacy is definitely not in the forefront of occupational choices for someone surviving in 1998. Creating rhythms with one's feet is actually misunderstood by the majority of our society and enjoyed by such a small and precious few. Sure, everyone loves listening to the intricate rhythms created by a mass of thundering feet, but few experience the intimate and individual expression of soul created through one's own soles.

I have spent the better part of 20 years enveloped in the world of auditory expression and the search for its meaning, its essence and its mysteries. I have experienced the rehearsals, the "bus and truck" tours, the master classes and the struggle to "make ends meet" while always asking *why?*

The Souls of Your Feet is my attempt to answer and share that question. I have been constantly asked by students and friends to write a manual on tap dance and it has always been my dream to write about life in general based on the concepts and lessons of rhythm and rhythmic expression. I do feel that the basic elements of communication are the same whether through tap dancing or writing an important document on a current world crisis. It's my opinion that *simplicity* and *listening* hold a basic truth. Know your language of communication, listen to your world and speak from your heart honestly and creation will be at your fingertips, or in this case, at your feet.

Tap dance is literally a language, an exquisite collection of sound and body and a strong voice of communication. It has its ABC's, its common words, its sentences and its paragraphs. Some collections of sound are traditional but most importantly they can be your own. Yes, you must practice in order to fully express yourself with this beautiful articulation but that is no different than mastering any other foreign tongue. When you do grasp the rein of rhythm, however, you'll never want to let go. Its inclusion in life is one of the most natural and vital ingredients to being human.

There's nothing more pure and significant than your own voice being sent out into the world, whether through the spoken word or through your feet.

Introduction

You and Your Feet

Tap dancing is a mode of transportation in the search for self-expression. Through the ages, humans have instinctively utilized their innate sense of rhythm to communicate with their world and each other through dancing. In fact, along with singing, this artform is expression in its purist sense. No external tools are needed for the basics of dance and the enjoyment of self-exploration; the rhythms you create can be all your own.

Having bought this book, however, you'll probably have more fun with some tap shoes (and it will make much more sense!). Not only can you hear your rhythmic creations, but you'll be able to share your voice with others. But here's your first lesson: *Know and remember, it's not about the shoes.* Your rhythms are created internally, your body moves the structures of "steps" and your feet bring the sounds to life outside of *you*. Without this internal connection, the shoes are useless. Understanding your voice makes it happen. Then, and only then, the shoes can make all the difference in the world!

What's the most important thing about tap?

Within this book, you will find one interpretation of the rhythms and structures that have been handed down to me by numerous individuals who lovingly shared their voice. You will also find new discoveries and explorations of the artform that I have developed through many years as a teacher, dancer and choreographer. This guidebook is, by no means, meant as a complete reference manual for tap dance. It will, however show you how my soul has defined a foundation for its voice through my feet. I will share these ideas and traditions that have helped my dancers, my students and myself enjoy this unique form of physical communication. In doing so, this guidebook will hopefully lead you to a place of pure rhythmic enjoyment!

Rhythm!

Within the following chapters, you will find the necessary tools to explore your inner rhythms and discover the hidden talents of your feet. You will also be introduced to the elements of weight placement and the basic fundamental sound structures to begin a strong foundation in the essentials of tap dancing. Utilize the easy-to-understand practice and play techniques throughout the guidebook to bring your rhythms, improvisations and/or choreography to life. Each basic step or combination of steps can be utilized in any order if you just want to play or if you already have a good technical foundation in tap. However, the guidebook is written in a developmental order to better serve the beginning student or teacher, not as a complete manual but a friendly guide for an incredible journey.

As with any form of dance, body awareness in tap is essential. You can strengthen this awareness for your explorations by also taking ballet, jazz, yoga or tai chi to reinforce your sense of balance and center. This guidebook will make no reference to the use of upper body movement unless crucial to uphold a tradition.

You can start your basics in Chapter One with or without tap shoes. Most exercises and structures are based on weight transfer and balance. If you're a beginner, you will find that these areas will need most of your attention. Tap shoes tend to make new dancers "hit" the floor rather than trusting and utilizing their legs and bodies. Remember: *It's not your feet that tap dance.* In fact, the two parts of your body that lead your rhythms are your ears and your hips!

What moves your feet?

The work of the total leg is a vital component in the theory of this book and my technique. In any dance form, the hips are actually the heart of all movement; wherever they go you go. If they travel so do your legs and if your legs travel so do your feet! If you're "over your hips" you can be grounded and balanced even if you travel across the floor.

. . .your hips!

All technical terms and definitions listed are based on weight placement and tone quality and in most cases will not require the notation of which foot is being used! Unless noted, you may begin right or left and the terms used will lead you from one foot to the other! *

* **Guidebook Note: Unfortunately, due to time constraints in the release of this book, I was not able to utilize an incredible tool of tap notation that partners my philosophies of movement wonderfully. In the absence of this reference within these pages, I would highly recommend utilizing this notation technique (that perhaps will be included in a second edition of this guidebook) entitled Kahnotation ©. This written collection of symbols was developed by the late tap dancer Stan Kahn and is currently utilized by his protege Sam Weber. This wonderful written method can be used as strong written foundation of tap technique and your creations. The strength of Kahnotation is the basics of weight transfer as is also the foundation of *The Souls of Your Feet*. (See Appendix — *Resources & Supplies.*)**

Utilize this book as if the pages were your tour guide on a wonderful, rhythmic journey. Use the reference sections and chapters as your maps to create your own individual excursion and get hints for your travels from the * Guidebook Notes *(as seen on page 22)*. Your individual freedom will lie in your own schedule, your own itinerary and your own time. Feel free to navigate your tour first with the referenced rhythms or, if you'd rather, with the basic definitions of sound. Either component can be your comprehension guide in that both are equally important. The simplified tap dance structure utilized within these pages will hopefully lead you to savor the experience and create your own variations with minimum "left brain activity."

Think of this journey in another way: Imagine learning how to sing a song in an unfamiliar foreign tongue. If you were coached and drilled in repetition, you could most likely sing it (and perhaps beautifully) if given enough time to practice. * In fact, you actually wouldn't have to know what you were singing about! But, fortunately not knowing does make a difference. Singing words you understand is the only way to truly communicate. Knowing your basics in tap is the only way to tap dance!

* **Guidebook Note: This rote learning process is actually a mainstream teaching tool in many dance studios. "Routines" are a large percentage of classroom work rather than technique. Imagine the difference if the dancers actually "spoke" the language.**

As another example, one of my dancers, many years ago, once used an image to define the process of learning tap choreography. He visualized himself standing in front of a wall of shelves, each symbolizing a tap step or figure. When trying to comprehend a tap combination, he envied the dancer able to file each new phrase easily within the categorized shelves, effortlessly catching the step like a ball and instinctively tossing it into the correct cubicle. *The Souls of Your Feet* is finally my soul's definition of those shelves in print. Most (if not all) tap choreography I've encountered can be categorized within the basic structures in this guidebook. Again, learn these basics, and most everything else is a variation!

Along with this book, I would also highly recommend any dancer exploring the art of tap to add to their library the following titles: *Jazz Dance* by Marshall and Jean Stearns, *Tap!* by Rusty E. Frank, *Footprints* by Peter Petronio (an incredible collection of black and white photos of not only tap dancers but their musicians), *Inside Tap* by Anita Feldman (for another soul's journey in tap), and *The Tap Dance Dictionary* and *Tap Roots* by Mark Knowles. I would also recommend joining the International Tap Association, reading Melba Huber's monthly tap article in *Dancer*, and going to see as many professional tap dancers and companies that you can *(see Appendix)*. And, last but not least, find at least one *Soul Mate* in a fellow tap dancer or musician — someone to converse with rhythmically.

Finally, communication and an understanding of your history, your world, your music and your language will bring you closer to this indigenous American artform and closer to your own individual, rhythmic voice. Take the time to discover the artists referenced throughout this book *(see Appendix)*. A rhythmic voice that is guided by a legacy of figures, steps and sounds, woven in a tapestry of individual souls singing their own unique melodies is the beauty in the ever-changing definition of tap.

Begin with the warm-up exercises and then continue to Chapter

One for a look at basic tap technique. After you've got your basics and basic variations "under your belt", travel next to the following chapters for a look into the soul of this guidebook: the fundamentals and tools of tap dance creations. Use the three reference guide sections: The Language of Tap, Rhythm & Music Structures and The Creation Five to help define your sounds and your technique along the way.

On your journey, remember to take your time, listen to your feet, improvise often and ask questions of those you respect. And, as Jimmy Slyde says, "keep dancin'!"

Reference Guide I
The Language of Tap

Soles

Terminology

The following is a list of terms and definitions that I utilize for my tap dance creations. This list can change drastically depending on the region of the country or the tap dance teacher one is studying with. This is however, a generalized collection that I find most utilized in the U.S. with some personalized additions. These terms are in common use order rather than alphabetical and are based in tone quality as well as weight placement.

Creating One Sound — The ABC's

STEP
The shifting of weight from one foot to the other as in walking. The weight is carried on the ball of the foot. The movement may be in any direction.

SINGLE
Same as a STEP

STAMP
A "step" on a flat foot (toe and heel simultaneously) and includes a transfer of weight.

TOUCH
While this movement can sound like a STEP and utilizes the ball of the foot, there is no change of weight.

STOMP
Sounds similar to a STAMP as the FLAT of the foot is used; however, there is no transfer of weight.

BRUSH (Front Brush)
Striking and leaving the floor with the forepart of the foot in a forward motion. This can be a short movement from the knee or (as this guidebook utilizes) an action from the hip. This basic can create sound with the ball of the foot as well as other surfaces of the toe tap to create different tone qualities.

BACK (Back Brush)
Same as BRUSH but striking the floor in a backward motion. Frequently called a "Spank."

SCUFF
Similar to a forward BRUSH striking the floor with the heel.

DIG
To "dig" the back of the heel of the free foot into the floor. This movement is usually slightly forward of the supporting leg.

HEEL
Executed by dropping the heel of a weight-bearing foot.

HEEL DROP
Executed by dropping the heel of a non-weight-bearing foot.

HEEL STEP
Stepping onto the heel only with a definite transfer of weight.

HEEL TAP
Similar to a DIG but the action is percussive and leaves the floor.

TOE
Dropping the toe of a weight-bearing foot.

TOE DROP
Dropping the toe of a non-weight-bearing foot.

TOE STAND
A move putting all the weight on the tip of the shoe.

PUNCH
Striking the floor with the tip of the shoe, often behind your standing leg but may be done in any direction. Also known as a "jab."

TOE TAP
Similar to a TOUCH but the action leaves the floor.

RIM SHOT
Striking the floor with the outside or inside of the heel usually crossing in front or behind the weight bearing leg.

HOP
"Hopping" on the ball of the foot with no transfer of weight.

HAMP
Same as HOP, but with a flat foot.

LEAP
A total transfer of weight on the ball of the foot with the transition airborne and both feet off the floor. This move does not have to travel as in a ballet "jeté" or be executed in a broad, big fashion. This basic is mostly utilized when speed is a factor with the basic STEP.

LAMP
Same as LEAP, but with a flat foot.

JUMP
In tap dancing, JUMP implies landing on both feet together or apart usually on the balls of the feet.

SLAM
Executed with a very relaxed action, a STOMP with a straight leg. Usually, there is no transfer of weight.

CHUG

The weight-bearing foot sliding forward and ending with a HEEL. (Also called a "buck.") This may also be done with both legs simultaneously.

PULL

The movement is opposite that of a CHUG. From the weight bearing foot, SLIDE backward on the ball of the foot.

PUSH

Similar to a CHUG but the heel does not strike the floor.

HEEL CLICK

With weight on the balls of both feet, twist and strike heels together. Can also be executed while airborne between a LEAP. See CUTOUT.

TOE CLICK

With weight on both heels, twist inward to strike toes. As with the HEEL CLICK, this basic can be airborne.

HEEL TOE CLIP

Heel crossing over and striking the toe of the weight bearing leg while balanced on the heel.

TOE HEEL CLIP

Same as HEEL TOE CLIP, but striking the toe behind the body on the heel of the weight-bearing leg while balanced on the toe. Also called a TRIP.

SLIDE

A traveling movement of one foot that "slides" over the floor in any direction with or without a transfer of weight and using any part of the foot. This can be the first sound of a WING or an independent   move of its own.

SCRAPE

To "scrape" the outside or inside edge of the toe tap across the floor.

DRAW

A movement of one foot over the floor from an open position (away from the body) to a closed position without a transfer of weight.

Creating Two Sounds

DOUBLE

Any BRUSH/STEP or BACK/STEP as well as with LEAPS.

SHUFFLE

The sounds produced are a BRUSH and a BACK. Basic technique isolates these as two distinct moves; advanced technique is one action with a relaxed ankle and action from the hip creating a BRUSH/TOE TAP.

SCUFFLE

Same as SHUFFLE but with a SCUFF and BACK.

BALL CHANGE (B/C)

Traditional movement in many forms of dance as well as tap. A rocking action of two quick "steps," usually STEP/STEP that keeps the weight bearing leg the same. All front, back and side positions are utilized. To go further, any rocking two sound transfer from one leg to the other can be referred to as a BALL/CHANGE.

Examples: STEP/STAMP or HEEL DROP/HEEL.

FLAP

Traditionally a BRUSH/STEP or BACK/STEP in any direction, although utilized as a syncopated action. Advanced dancers will (with action from the hip) produce a movement that closely resembles a BRUSH and a STEP to a straight leg. This action starts by "lifting" the knee from the hip and "dropping" the leg underneath your body.

FLAM
Named for a common drum rudiment this basic includes a TOUCH (on the inside or outside of the shoe) and a RIM SHOT done as one action.

SLAP
The action is like a FLAP, but there is no change of weight.

RIFF
A BRUSH (or TOUCH) and a SCUFF as one action.

BACK RIFF
DIG/BACK.

CUTOUT
A LEAP from one foot to the other with a HEEL CLICK in the air.

BASIC PULLBACK
Execute a DOUBLE (BACK/STEP) on both feet simultaneously.

BASIC PULLOVER
Execute a DOUBLE (BRUSH/STEP) on both feet simultaneously to travel front.

BASIC PULLSIDE
A DOUBLE (as a BACK/STEP or BRUSH/STEP) traveling sideways on both feet simultaneously.

PICKUP
A DOUBLE (BACK/STEP) on the weight-bearing leg.

PICKUP CHANGE
Adding a BACK while executing a LEAP.

PICKOVER
Adding a BRUSH while executing a HOP traveling forward.

PICKOVER CHANGE
Adding a BRUSH while executing a LEAP traveling forward.

ROLL
STEP/HEEL.

REVERSE ROLL
HEEL STEP/TOE.

PADDLE
DIG/BACK (Same as Reverse Riff).

BASIC CRAWL
STEP/HEEL/TOE turning in or out.

BASIC CRAMP
JUMP/HEEL with both feet.

FLEA-HOP
Actually a SLIDE away from with the weight bearing foot toward a
STEP or LEAP transfer.

TRENCH
A LEAP from foot to foot that includes a sliding (as a ronde de jambe)
movement of the supporting foot as in the action of a speed skater. The
weight-bearing foot is the opposite of that used in a FLEA-HOP.
* See Chapter Four — The B.S. Chorus

Creating Three Sounds

TRIPLE
SHUFFLE/STEP or SHUFFLE/LEAP.

BASIC ESSENCE
STEP/BALL/CHANGE crossing front.
* See Chapter Two — The Essence & Waltz Clog

BOMBERSHAY
STEP/BACK/HEEL STEP.
* See Chapter Two — Bombershays

BASIC DRAWBACK
BRUSH/HEEL/STEP.
* See Chapter Two — Drawbacks

BASIC DRAWFRONT
Same as DRAWBACK goin' the other way!

ONE & 1/2
Straight leg SHUFFLE with an added BACK or TOE TAP.

OPEN THIRD
Execute a SHUFFLE but allow the heel to SCUFF or TAP between
the BRUSH and the BACK. A very relaxed ankle is essential. Sometimes referred to as a "riffle."

CLOSED THIRD
Execute a FLAP but allow the heel to TAP between the BRUSH and the
STEP or TOE DROP. Very relaxed and thrown. Is also called a "Slurp."

3 point CRAWL *(See Basic CRAWL.)*
The most basic CRAWL. Inverted STEP/HEEL/TOE "crawling" across
the floor with the first sound executed with a turned-in leg. This basic

can also be non-weight bearing: TOUCH/HEEL DROP/TOE DROP.
* *See Chapter Two — Crawls*

RIP
BRUSH/PICKUP CHANGE *(See TREADMILL).*

BACK RIP
A BACK/PICKOVER CHANGE combined.

RIFFLE
Execute a RIFF with the free foot, adding a HEEL with the supporting foot. Some dancers use this term for what I call a THIRD.

BASIC WING
A three sound JUMP variation adding a relaxed BRUSH outward on the side of the feet, then BACK inward with the inside or tip of the shoes landing on the BALLS of both feet. This is also a TRIPLE.
* *See Chapter Two — Pullbacks, Pickups & Wings*

SINGLE WING
The same as above but a HOP variation executed on the single weight-bearing leg.

SWAP
A total transfer of weight is involved replacing the HOP of a Single WING with a LEAP.

TREADMILL (or RIP)
BRUSH/PICKUP CHANGE.

Creating Four Sounds

QUADRUPLE
SHUFFLE (executed with a straight leg)/BACK/STEP. Some teachers refer to a TRIPLE with a HEEL as a "Quadruple." This guidebook

definition is based on the traditional SINGLE, DOUBLE and TRIPLE being all weight transfers on the ball of the foot.

IRISH
SHUFFLE/HOP/STEP. This step is traditionally executed crossing either front or back behind the supporting leg. I personally use this step in neutral. When crossing, I refer to it either as a "Front Irish" or "Back Irish".
* See Chapter One — Basic Figures

PADDLE & ROLL
Exactly as it sounds: a PADDLE and a ROLL. Also referred to as a "paradiddle."
* See Chapter Two — The Paddle & Roll

4 POINT RIFF WALK
TOUCH/SCUFF/DIG/TOE.
* See Chapter Two — Riffs & Riff Walks

CRAMP ROLL
STEP/STEP/HEEL/HEEL. RLRL or LRLR.
*See Chapter Two — Cramp Rolls

"Double" PULLBACK
BACK/BACK/STEP/STEP. Usually executed as one action as with a CRAMP ROLL. RLRL or LRLR.
* See Chapter Two — Pullbacks, Pickups & Wings

"Double" PULLOVER
Same as above replacing the BACKS with BRUSHES to the front.

"Double" FLAP
Two FLAPS executed as one action.

"Double" SHUFFLE
Yep, you guessed it . . . two SHUFFLES.

"Double" TOE PUNCH
Execute two TOE PUNCHES in the order of a CRAMP ROLL.
PUNCH/PUNCH/STEP/STEP (RLRL or LRLR)

BASIC MAXI FORD or MAXI
SHUFFLE/LEAP/PUNCH. The PUNCH traditionally crosses back. I
actually learned this step starting with an initial STEP before the
SHUFFLE for five sounds. I discovered, however, its kissing cousin is
the GRABOFF.
* See Chapter Two — Maxi's & Graboffs*

BASIC GRABOFF
SHUFFLE/LEAP/STEP. Instead of the PUNCH as in the MAXI, you
STEP on your final sound. This final STEP can cross either front or
back. Traditional version executes the LEAP as a PICKUP CHANGE.
In many regions, the term "Graboff" is also used for a   SHUFFLE/
PICKUP CHANGE.

SINGLE BUFFALO
STEP/SHUFFLE/STEP traveling toward the first sound (and to the
side) ending with free leg bent and crossing front to repeat. That's "sur
le cou de pied" if you're taking ballet!

Creating Five Sounds

QUINTUPLET
"Double" SHUFFLE/STEP.

BASIC WALTZ CLOG
STEP/SHUFFLE B/C traditionally crossing the B/C back or front.
* See Chapter Two — The Essence & Waltz Clog*

GRABROLL
SHUFFLE/PICKUP CHANGE/HEEL.

FIVE SOUND WING
"Double" SHUFFLE/STEP on both legs at the same time. Sheeeeeeeesh.
* See Chapter Two — Pullbacks, Pickups & Wings

SINGLE FIVE SOUND WING
Now do it on one leg!

FIVE SOUND SWAP
Now land on the other leg by replacing the STEP with a LEAP! Also known as The Condos Wing.

NERVE TAP
A fast series of TAPS (either toe or heel) executed with a tense leg and relaxed ankle. Can actually be as many counts as needed.

Creating Basic Floor Patterns

BASIC GRAPEVINE
A series of eight STEPS traveling to the side in a crossing formation: to the side, back, side, front, side, back, side TOUCH. Some teachers choose to start crossing front first rather than back.

BASIC JAZZ SQUARE
A series of four STEPS that diagram a box or square under your body. Start with the first STEP crossing the standing leg, STEP to the back, STEP to the side and then STEP to the front. All steps are made within the corners of an imaginary square. To change sides, adjust your final STEP to a TOUCH and start your next JAZZ SQUARE to the opposite side.

BASIC PADDLE-TURN
A traditional "soft shoe" figure that utilizes a series of STEP B/C's that turn to the inside or outside of your supporting leg. This figure traditionally takes up one BAR of 4/4 music.
* *See Chapter Two — The Essence & Waltz Clog*

BASIC SUSIE-Q
A traditional two sound action of "winding" a turned-in working leg across your body with a HEEL STEP and "unwinding" to turnout by pivoting on your heel and finishing with a STEP.
* *See Chapter Two — Bombershays*

BASIC STAR
A series of three BRUSH/TOUCH B/C's finishing with a BRUSH/STEP B/C. Execute to four positions starting to the front then side then back and finishing to the side. Repeat on the other side to complete the diagram of a five point star. All B/C's are executed with heels.
* *See Chapter Two — The Star*

BASIC CRAWL
A three sound figure that starts with a turned-in "pigeon-toed" STEP followed by a turned-out HEEL and TOE.
* *See Chapter Two — Crawls*

TURNS
Numerous turns can be utilized as basic floor patterns in tap dance to include chainés, pirouettes, pencil, barrel, pivot, skaters, piqués and many more. Tap figures and basics that have been used traditionally as turns include cramp rolls, Jimmy crawls (commonly known as "rhythm turns"), pendulum wings, Maxi's, riffs, and of course SINGLES, DOUBLES and TRIPLES in numerous variations.

OBIKABBIBLE
This is "the Wizard of Oz step." A "kick" BALL/CHANGE/LEAP with the first sound of the B/C crossing in front of the standing leg and the LEAP traveling to the side of the body in the direction of the kick. (a1a2)

Reference Guide II

The Creation Five

Creation

The Creation Five

Based on a full body concept of tap dance, I have developed reference movements relative to the hip and the execution of all tap sounds, giving the dancer a basic core from which to dance. These Creation Five concepts can simplify all movement covered in this book.

Fall

Movement that shifts your full weight letting your body *"fall"* into the floor.

Examples: STEP, LEAP, HEEL.

Drop

Movement that is motivated by *"dropping"* your leg to the floor without a transfer of full body weight.

Examples: TOUCH, DIG, PUNCH.

Pull

Movement that requires *"pulling"* your leg from your hip.

Examples: BACK, SHUFFLES before BALL CHANGES, PULL-BACKS.

Throw

Movement that requires *"throwing"* your leg from your hip.

Examples: Most SHUFFLES, SCUFF, THIRDS.

Lift

Movement that requires "*lifting*" your leg.
Examples: Preparations for movement and end of a PUNCH.

The basic fundamental structure of the Creation Five is the utilization of your hips and legs when you tap dance and the knowledge of where your body is "standing" and balanced when making sounds. The use of this simple theory is greatly beneficial in finding the simple movement structure or "skeleton" step in all tap movement. Now, if you're a beginner, all of this will soon make sense as you become familiar with the terms and definitions being used in this guidebook. If you have tap experience, you will have hopefully discovered a new "toy"!

Reference Guide III

Rhythm & Music Structures

Time

The Structures of Time

Whether tap dancing or playing a musical instrument, it is always important to understand the structures of time, tempo and rhythm. Without this knowledge, you can only guess at the relationship you hold to your rhythmic voice and your accompaniment.

The heartbeat of all of our work as tap dancers is the underscoring pattern of pulses we call **BEATS.** A BEAT can be defined as a regular and repeating pattern that is the basic unit of time in music. This regular pattern enables musicians (as tap dancers are!) to "keep time" with their own rhythms while staying connected to this core structure.

To illustrate a basic rhythm structure, you can utilize the following simple tune where there is a solid BEAT going on while you sing. It's this BEAT that keeps you knowing where the next note will fall.

Twinkle		Twinkle		Little		Star	
1	2	**3**	4	**1**	2	**3**	4
How	I	Wonder		What	You	Are	
1	2	**3**	4	**1**	2	**3**	4

Now, notice the division of the fours BEATS as well as the counts that have been marked in bold. The divisions are known as BARS or MEASURES that divide (in this case) the music into equal parts of four (4/4 TIME). The bold BEATS of 1 and 3 within each BAR are known as the DOWNBEATS; the 2's and 4's are known as the UP-BEATS. All of the BEATS in this case are also known as **QUARTER NOTES**.

If you divide these BEATS even further by adding OFFBEATS, you now have **EIGHTH NOTES** as a DUPLE feel.

1   &   2   &   **3**   &   4   &

or

You now have **EIGHTH NOTES** as a TRIPLET feel.

1   a   2   a   **3**   a   4   a

If you add another OFFBEAT between, you now have complete **TRIPLETS**.

1   &   a   2   &   a   **3**   &   a   4   &   a

If once again, you now have **SIXTEENTH NOTES**.

1   e   &   a   2   e   &   a   **3**   e   &   a   4   e   &   a

For further understanding, here is another visual method to show these relationships keeping the DOWNBEATS in bold.

1

Whole Note

1   3

Half Notes

1 2 **3** 4
Quarter Notes

1 & 2 & **3** & 4 &
Eighth Notes — Duple Feel or Straight

1 a 2 a **3** a 4 a
Eighth Notes — Triplet Feel or Syncopated

1 e & a 2 e & a **3** e & a 4 e & a
Sixteenth Notes

1 & a 2 & a **3** & a 4 & a
Triplets

Most of us were taught some sort of counting method similar to this in elementary school and there are more ways of vocally counting these divisions. *Example:* "ah & a 1 ah & a 2" for SIXTEENTH NOTES. The version listed in the previous diagram seems most often used by tap dancers to clarify basic rhythms.

Also, many individuals are taught as dancers to count to 8 to successfully feel the phrasing of dance combinations and choreography. I feel, however, that this creates a limitation and confusion to the actual meter being played. *

* **Guidebook Note: When working with any jazz musicians, they'll definitely look at you funny if you don't know your music. When you put on a pair of tap shoes** *you too are a musician!* **Speak the language and share the artform with mutual respect.**

Definitions of Time & Music

BEAT
A regular and repeating pattern that is the basic unit of time in music.

DOWNBEATS
1 and 3 in a BAR of 4 BEATS. The strongest pulse within the structure.

UPBEATS
2 and 4 in a BAR of 4 BEATS.

BAR or **MEASURE**
An equal division of BEATS for the purpose of reading and counting music.

OFFBEAT
The BEATS between the primary notes (i.e. 1234) in a BAR of music. *Example:* &1 (& is the OFFBEAT).

The following are additional definitions that are also needed to comprehend basic musical structures:

DOUBLE TIME
Doubling a rhythm pattern within its original BAR structure.

1		2		**3**		4	
1	2	**3**	4	1	2	**3**	4

(DOUBLE TIME)

SYNCOPATION
A rhythm that accents or stresses the OFFBEAT or UPBEATS. An irregular rhythm pattern as in Swinging (or TRIPLET) Eighth Notes.

SWING

Accenting the OFFBEAT rather than the DOWNBEATS. This element is also considered SYNCOPATED as in Swing Music.

SHADING

The dynamics of accent, tone and volume within your tap voice. This is what separates the students from the masters.

TEMPO

The rate of speed at which BEATS occur in music.

REST

No sound is made. For the purpose of notation, ( ) will be used around BEATS that do not make sound. *Example:* **1** &(2) **3** &

ACCENT

To emphasize or stress a note or series of notes within music.

Common Time Signatures

Time signatures are used by musicians as guides for the division of BEATS in each BAR. (Remember, the strong bold BEATS are the DOWNBEATS.)

4/4 Four QUARTER NOTES in a BAR
|**1**   2   **3**   4|

2/4 Two QUARTER NOTES in a BAR
|**1**   2|

3/4   Three QUARTER NOTES in a BAR **(Waltz Time)**

|1   2   3|

6/8   Six EIGHTH NOTES in a BAR

|1   2   3   4   5   6|

Many more time signatures exist, but for the purpose of this guidebook I will keep this element of music simple. *

* Guidebook Note: Anita Feldman's *Inside Tap* is an excellent source of time signature, rhythm and meter explorations and knowledge! *(See Appendix.)*

Phrase & Chorus Structure

The following definitions are used when defining additional divisions or sections of music:

PHRASE
In standard Western music, this term is used for a collection of 8 BARS.

CHORUS
In standard music also, this term is used for a collection of 4 PHRASES
— a total of 32 BARS.

BRIDGE
The third PHRASE in a standard tune of AABA format where A symbolizes the same melody for 8 BARS and B symbolizes the 8 BAR BRIDGE between the A's.

STANDARD TUNE or **SIMPLE DANCE**
Two to three CHORUSES of music.

INTRODUCTION
A common collection of BARS (usually 2, 4 or 8) at the beginning of a song that leads into the HEAD or main melody.

TAG
An add-on ending (usually 2, 4 or 8 BARS) at the end of a CHORUS or song.

HEAD
A jazz term that defines the melody or main theme of a song when improvising.

VAMP
An even, pulsing BEAT or collection of BEATS that hold a melodic idea in preparation for a returning soloist.

STOP TIME
An even pulse of DOWNBEATS usually on count 1 of every two BARS adding the 3 for accent or the return of the melody line. This will usually also hold the chord progressions of the melody.

TACIT
Complete silence within music.

A CAPELLA
A term commonly used when dancing or singing without music.

BLUES CHORUS
An American music tradition that uses 3 sets of 4 BAR PHRASES to complete a CHORUS.

IMPROVISATION
The heart of jazz where the artist is free to spontaneously "make up" their music. As a tap dancer, this holds the freedom to play and explore!

CHOREOGRAPHY
A structured sequence of dance movement for the purpose of showing motivation, emotion or visual music.

Warm-up

Finding Your Hips & Legs

Presence

Finding Your Legs

This section will introduce to you a basic warm-up exercise that helps you find your placement as well as work on balance and relaxation.

First, take the time to stretch your calves. They're about to get a workout! You're going to spend a tremendous amount of time on the balls of your feet and, if you're a beginner, it's not the most natural place to be.

* Guidebook Note: All of the following exercises in this section are notated in an even rhythm for a purpose. Control and balance are only gained by a slow to moderate tempo and faithful repetition.

Exercise #1 – Stand in a neutral position, flatfooted. Feel your weight equally balanced on both legs and with your upper body "pulled up" out of your hips. Now, rock your weight to the *balls of your feet* lifting your heels off the floor. Now, this position is not as high as relevé in other forms of dance and it's actually where a ballet teacher won't let you balance! Tap dancers, however, utilize this position to keep the heel off the floor and not always for a classical and visual "line" of the leg.

* Guidebook Note: This does not mean body "line" and classical training are not important to tap dance. In fact, those dancers with ballet, jazz and/or modern training can become stronger tap dancers to train and more pleasing to the eyes of an audience as well as more adaptable to versatile tap choreography.

Now, stay there and gently pulse for a couple of minutes. Yes, I said minutes (not seconds). You'll start to feel all of the tiny muscles in your feet that you never use as well as your calf muscles. In this simple exercise, you're working on the gift and the nemesis of tap dance: **Balance**. The bane of many a beginner, this basic will take the most practice to perfect.

Exercise #2 – Stand again in your neutral position. Lift your right leg in front of you from the hip. Let your knee follow by bending and allow your calf and foot to relax. You should now be standing in a relaxed marching position. Be sure your ankle is also totally relaxed and without tension. The only muscles that should be working are your hip flexor (that little tiny muscle under your hip bone) and your standing leg. For help, imagine you have a string attached to your knee that's also attached to the ceiling and your leg is following in a reaction to this string being pulled like a marionette.

Now, release your leg to a straight 45-degree angle in front of your body keeping everything relaxed except your quadricep muscle (that big muscle on the top of your thigh) that's keeping your leg off the floor. Your knee should now be perfectly straight — so straight it may feel "locked." If you're successful in this action, you now have a straight leg. Now, try again and you will notice your ankle gently bouncing in rhythm as you straighten.

Try this exercise in three directions for 8 counts each, then 4, then 2, then finally for one. Drop your leg back to the floor on the final count of the last repetition to switch legs: Front, Side, Back & Side ("en croix" – as in the sign of a cross) always initiating the movement from your hip and not your knee.

(l-lift, t-throw, d-drop) — *Example (first eight counts):*

& **1** & 2 & **3** & 4 & | **1** & 2 & **3** 4
l   t   l   t l   t l   t l   t l   t   l   t   d

This exercise is developed for balance on the standing leg and to totally relax the working leg's foot and knee. In later work, this will become the motivation for DOUBLES, TRIPLES, QUADRUPLES, QUINTUPLETS, SHUFFLES, FLAPS, SLAPS and THIRDS.

Now, on to the basics . . .

Chapter One
The ABC's & The Basics

Purpose

Start with your ABC's . . .

The ABC's are the basic sounds created by the different and distinct parts of your foot. *(See Definitions & Terms — Creating One Sound.)* Each sound has its own execution and tone quality to help express and create the accent and dialect of your own special rhythmic voice. All feet can create these sounds but each individual will always sound unique!

In this section, you will discover and create some of the ABC's as well as basic combinations of these sounds used in tap dance.

Singles, Doubles & Triples

All of the following tap dance elements have two things in common: They are all executed with the *ball of the foot* and they all transfer your full weight from one leg to the other.

Step (SINGLE)

This is the basic foundation of all other tap dance executions. This is the actual vehicle of transportation that shifts your weight from one foot to the other. The most important aspect of this basic is staying on the ball of your foot.

Exercise #3 – Find a moderate tempo song you enjoy and shift your weight on each DOWNBEAT. Shift from side to side (or let your weight *"Fall"* as mentioned within the Creation 5) while executing a STEP from one leg to the other keeping your weight balanced and "on top" of the standing leg. After this feels comfortable try moving around the room and add the basic floor patterns of the GRAPEVINE and JAZZ SQUARE. Remember, your heels never come down.

Brush Step (DOUBLE)

By swinging your relaxed leg (and ankle) from your hip, strike a crisp sound on the ball of your foot to extend *(Creation 5 "Throw")* out from the front of your body. If you are using tap shoes, this action will create sound on the back part of your toe tap. This action to the front will create a front BRUSH. Now prepare your relaxed leg to the front and swing your foot to the back of your body again using your entire leg from the hip to strike the floor *(Creation 5 "Pull")*. You are now creating a BACK brush. Both of these executions are traditionally called "BRUSHES" and are front and/or back relative to your leg and not your body. For instance, you can execute a front BRUSH to the side of your body or a BACK brush crossing over your supporting leg. The terms BRUSH and BACK simplify the actions for this guidebook to reference each direction. Now add a STEP to a BRUSH or BACK and you've created a DOUBLE.

Exercise #4 – Add this BRUSH to your Exercise #3 utilizing the following rhythm pattern first with a front BRUSH then with the BACK brush.

BRUSH/STEP or BACK/STEP
& **1** & 2 & **3** & 4
(repeat tons of times)

Shuffle Step (TRIPLE)

Here we will combine a front BRUSH and a BACK brush to create a SHUFFLE. To start, keep your SHUFFLES at a relaxed diagonal from your body (around the 1:00 position). Again, swing your entire, relaxed leg to execute correctly. Your knee will bend as you move, but the motivation should be with your full leg movement as in *"Throw."* Swing or *"Pull"* your BACK brush toward your body (this is a hip action with the knee reacting naturally) to STEP underneath yourself to create a TRIPLE. The STEP action can actually happen anywhere on the floor, but for now should be executed in this simple fashion. When proficiency is acquired the (front) BRUSH/BACK (brush) action is replaced often by a BRUSH/TOE TAP.

Exercise #5 – Practice your TRIPLE in the following pattern first in place, then traveling to the front and then to the back.

> SHUFFLE/STEP
> &a1   &a2   &a3   &a4
> *(repeat also tons of times)*

* Guidebook Note: Full leg motivation is one of many different styles of tap technique. Many excellent tap dancers motivate their movements from their knees and ankles. However, my teaching and dancing style is based in the movement of the entire body and utilizes a relaxed action of the leg from the hips as in Exercise #2. The more advanced you become with this technique, in fact, the more you will be asked to actually dance with straight relaxed legs rather than bent in plié (with bent knees) as many teachers train. This does not mean that you don't bend your knees. On the contrary, your knees will bend at times when transferring your weight! Your knees, however, are not initiators of the sounds and action.

More Basic Figures

The Ball Change (B/C)

This traditional rocking step is a standard in all jazz-based dance forms. It consists of two STEPS but no full weight change for tap dance in most cases. It can utilize most of the ABC's but at this time will only consist of the two basic STEPS. You will not totally shift your weight thus staying on the same supporting leg. The following exercise will use the B/C in a back to front action.

Exercise #6 – SHUFFLE B/C, DOUBLE B/C to travel front in the diagram of a tree with the SHUFFLES creating limbs and the BRUSH and B/C's creating the trunk.

& **1** & 2 & **3** & 4
(again, repeat tons of times)

The Irish (The SINGLE Irish)

This traditional tap step is actually a derivative of Irish Step Dance. We've actually Americanized it quite a bit, but the basic is the same: SHUFFLE/HOP/STEP. (Actually, that's a "Rally Hop Step" in Irish.) In its traditional tap rhythm, this is a syncopated step (a1a2) but we will start with a controlled, even rhythm that strengthens the foundation of relaxation and balance.

Exercise #7 – SHUFFLE/HOP/STEP, SHUFFLE/HOP/STEP
SHUFFLE/HOP/STEP, SHUFFLE B/C

&1&2 &3&4 &1&2 &3&4 *(yep, keep repeating)*

Variations on the Basics

Now, if you're feeling comfortable and have found your relaxed and balanced center on the balls of your feet, you are ready for some variations. Here is a list of simple concepts and variations that will add spice to your basics and will lead to variations on all levels.

- **One & 1/2** – Straight leg SHUFFLE (BRUSH/TOE TAP) with an added BACK. *(See Warm-up.)*

- **Quadruple** – SHUFFLE with a straight leg extended as in the Warm-up, utilize the bounce of your relaxed ankle as the second sound. Add a BACK/STEP. Four sounds with one change of weight.

- **Quintuplet** – "Double" SHUFFLE/STEP. Five sounds with one weight change. *

* Guidebook Note: "Double", in this case, means to repeat twice. I'm utilizing the same word as with DOUBLE but both are completely different actions. "Double" is based on traditional terminology that has been used with tap for years for repeating twice.

- **Combinations** – Mix and match the above basics to create your own 8 BARS. Then try 16 and then a 32 BAR CHORUS. Many great steps can be created with the basics we've talked about so far like SHUFFLE/HOP/DOUBLE.

- **Rhythm Changes** – Try keeping the structures of the basics the same while matching the rhythm of a favorite song or nursery rhyme. A fun and challenging one is repeating SHUFFLE B/C,

DOUBLE B/C in the rhythm of Humpty Dumpty. Remember a DOUBLE is a BRUSH/STEP or BACK/STEP.

- **Add-a-Heel** – Try your SINGLES, DOUBLES and TRIPLES with HEELS!

- **Double-Up** – A wonderful idea based on the work of the late Steve Condos. Do everything twice. To Double-up an IRISH you would execute SHUFFLE/SHUFFLE/HOP/HOP/*TOUCH*/ STEP keeping the integrity of the weight change; however, try a "Double-up" literally with the terms and you'll end up with a whole different step (in this case, an Irish variation that doesn't switch sides!)

- **Graduate or S/D/T/Q/Q** – Turn a SINGLE into a DOUBLE or a DOUBLE into a TRIPLE or perhaps a QUINTUPLET. If you've learned a SINGLE IRISH . . . what's a DOUBLE IRISH?

* Guidebook Note: Remember what the SINGLE, DOUBLE & TRIPLE have in common: transfer of weight on the ball of the foot! For those of you with tap experience, this "graduation" is not referring to the Traditional Double Irish which is SHUFFLE/HOP/STEP/SHUFFLE B/C. For some reason, this tradition is neither a DOUBLE nor two IRISHES!

Now, with a grasp of the basics of sound (and some fun variations!), we will travel to some of the most common figures and patterns in tap dance as well as some of my own. I will introduce the basic structures, give you many more creative ideas based on these "steps" and give you many variations in which to play — all of which can be cross-referenced and used for any and all tap creations!

For the rest of this book, however, you will mostly be on your own for inventive rhythms and exercises. It is not my intention to have this written work replace your teacher and/or *your* creative mind. It is one thing to translate another's steps from paper to your feet, but the real *soul* of tap comes from within and utilizing the tools of the trade: **the basics** and traditions of sound and rhythm.

Most (if not all) basics are here for you within the chapters and the reference areas of this guidebook. The tradition of sound and rhythm is found in the music you love to listen to! The combination of both, with a strong history in jazz, is the tradition that has led you to this book and the magic of tap.

Remember again . . . *it's not about the steps.* As with any spoken language, tap is communication. Utilize this written gift from me, this one soul's adventure truly as a *guidebook* and **find your own voice.**

The only rule: **Have something to say.**

Enjoy your continued journey.

Chapter Two
Rhythmic
"Words" & Figures

Rhythm

The Star

This Acia Basic is comprised of BRUSH/TOUCH B/C as an en croix (again, referring to the diagram of a cross) series starting with one leg and repeating on the other to complete a diagram of a five point "star" on the floor. The B/C is composed, in this case, of two heels: the first without weight as a DROP and the second on your standing leg as a HEEL. The change of weight will occur on your final execution or fourth repetition in which the TOUCH will be replaced with a STEP.

(BRUSH/TOUCH/HEEL DROP/HEEL) 2x *(Front & side)*
   (a1a2a3a4)

BACK/TOUCH/HEEL DROP/HEEL *(Crossing back)*
   (a1 a2)

BRUSH/STEP/HEEL DROP/HEEL *(Switching weight to the side)*
   (a3 a4)

Repeat on the other leg to complete the STAR. *(Again, remember this is an en croix series - front, side, back, side.)*

Variations

- **The Broadway** – Add a BACK/HEEL/PUNCH (crossing behind standing leg)/HEEL to the weight change element of the Star (last four beats). Also referred to as "In the Mood" and "The Shirley Temple." *
  (a1a2a3a4)

* **Guidebook Note: I actually referred to The Broadway as an "In the Mood" until very recently. Tap dance writer Melba Huber enlightened my version by reminding me that the step came way before the song!**

- **Star Directions** – Change or repeat BRUSH/TOUCH B/C in any and all directions.

- **Triplet Star** – Add an initial HEEL on your standing leg before each B/C.
  (a1&a2)

- **Rhythm Changes** – Play with different rhythms and melodies keeping the basic footwork the same.

- **Shuffle Star** – Replace the BRUSHES with SHUFFLES. Can also be thought of as a TRIPLE STAR. *

* **Guidebook Note: The first sound of a BALL CHANGE is also taken as a weight change with regard to SINGLES, DOUBLES, TRIPLES and so on.**

- **One & 1/2 Star** – Replace the BRUSHES with One & 1/2's.

- **Double-Up Star** – Double all sounds to create another figure. Hint: A relaxed and hip motivated SHUFFLE will replace the BRUSHES and BACKS.

- **Heel/Toe Replacements** – Change TOUCHES to DIGS and HEELS to TOES.

Crawls

This basic figure is comprised of a turned-in (pigeon-toed) STEP, a turned-out (from the hip) HEEL with an added TOE creating 3 sounds. You can also start turned-in and reverse the direction. This figure is utilized also on a weight-bearing leg by starting with a TOE. To create a 4, 5, 6 or more CRAWL you continue to the next sound in sequence and travel toward or away from the working leg across the floor. Numerous variations can come from this versatile basic as shown by Ms. Brenda Bufalino whose famous "Swampscott Crawl" is among many of her wonderful manipulations.

(STEP - s/ HEEL - h / TOE - t)

&	1	&	or	1	&	2
s	h	t		s	h	t

- **4 Point Crawl**
  (&1&2)

- **5 Point Crawl**
  (&1&2&)

- **6 Point Crawl**
  (&1&2&3)

Variations

- **Paddle & Roll** – Combinations with this figure lead to exciting creations. Utilize all the Paddle & Roll variations also!

Riffs & Riff Walks

A basic RIFF is comprised of a TOUCH/SCUFF or BRUSH/ SCUFF. Following is a list of common standing RIFFS and RIFF WALKS. As with all tap figures, these basics can be executed in any rhythm. *

* Guidebook Note: Most traditional figures go hand-in-hand with traditional rhythms, however, many new ideas come from changing rhythm alone!

Standing Riffs

Unlike the RIFF WALKS, these figures do not change weight.

- **Basic Riff** – TOUCH/SCUFF or BRUSH/SCUFF.

- **Reverse Riff** – DIG/BACK (also a PADDLE).

- **3 Point** – Add a HEEL to the basic RIFF. I also call this a RIFFLE. Many dancers refer to an OPEN THIRD as a RIFFLE. (&a1)

- **4 Point** – Add a HEEL before the 3 Point. (4&a1)

- **5 Point** – Add a DIG to the end of the 4 Point. (&4&a1)

- **6 Point** – Add a TOE DROP to the end of the 5 Point. (&a4&a1)

- **7 Point** – Add a HEEL on the working leg at the end of the 6 Point.

  (e&a4&a1)

- **8 Point** – Add a HEEL DROP on the working leg before the final HEEL of the 7 Point.

  (e&a4e&a1)

  All of the 3-8 Point RIFFS can be executed also with the RE-VERSE RIFF.

Riff Walks

These are common figures utilized as an intricate, close-to-the-floor pattern with one weight shift as in walking. (I believe I was actually unconsciously practicing riffs, at 8 years old, when my Mom said "quit draggin' your feet!")

- **4 Point** – RIFF/DIG (In this case with a change of weight) * TOE.

  (&1&2)

- **5 Point (on one foot)** – Add a HEEL to the 4 Point.

  (a1&a2)

* **Guidebook Note: The weight transfer actually starts with the heel (as a DIG) and is completed on the TOE. Defining this shift with a HEEL STEP can actually be confusing and make the next weight shift more difficult.**

- **5 Point (on two feet)** – The basic for the next 6 RIFF WALKS. RIFF/HEEL/DIG (w/weight)/TOE.

  (a1&a2)

- **6 Point** – Add a HEEL to the 5 Point.
  (&a1&a2)

- **7 Point** – Replace the last HEEL in a 6 Point with a B/C (HEEL DROP/HEEL).
  (e&a1&a2)

- **8 Point** – Add a TOE to a 7 Point.
  (e&a1e&a2)

- **9 Point** – This as actually one of my own. Execute a 7 Point rotating the B/C HEELS toward the front of your body then adding an additional B/C with TOES in the same forward and rotating fashion.
  (4e&a1e&a2)

- **10 Point** – Also an Acia creation. Add a CHUG to the end of the 9 Point.
  (4e&a1e&a2**3**)

- **11 Point** – A common figure that is not always referred to as a RIFF but should be. 3 Point RIFF/DIG/BACK/HEEL (crossing your supporting leg), and then a 5 Point RIFF WALK (two feet).
  (a1&a2&a**3**&a4)

- **12 Point** – Add a HEEL to the end of the 11 Point.
  (&a1&a2&a**3**&a4)

Variations

- **In Succession** – After successfully memorizing these RIFFS and RIFF WALKS, try executing them in order with an even rhythm. This is actually more difficult than it sounds due to the even pulse of the BAR and the uneven count of the continuation of the RIFFS. After trying even timing, try a simple syncopation (a1a2a3a4 . . .) or a melody line.

- **Rhythm Changes** – All RIFFS & RIFF WALKS can and should be done with any rhythm you want. Try rests within the rhythm structure chosen and thus create a new one!

- **Accent Changes** – A variation for all figures. Accent a normally weak beat or non-weight-bearing sound.

- **Add-Ons** – Attach your RIFFS and/or RIFF WALKS to Basic Structures such as SINGLES, DOUBLES, TRIPLES & IRISHES.

  Example: SHUFFLE B/C, 5 PT (Walking)
  (a1a2a3&a4)

- **Backwards** – All RIFFS begin with the toe (in this case a TOUCH). Try reversing all of the RIFFS following the example of REVERSE RIFF. Hint: All of the weight changes in the RIFF WALKS will be STEPS rather than DIGS (w/weight) and all of the HEELS and TOES will reverse.

Comparison Example #1
4 Pt RIFF/W - TOUCH/SCUFF/DIG (w/weight)/TOE

Comparison Example #2
4 Pt REV RIFF/W - DIG/BACK/STEP/HEEL

I actually introduce the 4 Point RIFF/WALK and the PADDLE & ROLL (*Comparison Example #2*) together as the latter *is* the REVERSE 4 Point RIFF WALK.

Drawbacks

This term refers to a basic figure comprised of a BACK/HEEL/STEP commonly executed in a triplet rhythm. This was a favorite of our old B/W classic movie dancers like Ann Miller and Eleanor Powell.

- **SINGLE Drawback** – BACK/HEEL/STEP.
  (a1 2)

- **DOUBLE Drawback** – Replace the STEP or SINGLE with a DOUBLE.
  (a1a2)

- **TRIPLE Drawback** (Basic Cincinnati) – Replace the DOUBLE with a TRIPLE.
  (a1&a2)

Variations

- **Drawfront** – Change the BACK to a BRUSH.

- **The Spanish Crawl** – Cross leg over leg in the execution of a SINGLE DRAWBACK starting with the initial BACK. This pattern will reverse crossing legs on *every other* repetition. Traditionally, the crossing is started on the second repetition.

- **Crossing S/D/T/Q/Q** – Keeping the pattern of the Spanish Crawl or continually crossing over with each execution. Hint: SHUFFLE and BACK (or BRUSH) with your relaxed and extended leg *in the direction* of your next weight change.

- **Walkin' to Church** – Replace the BRUSH with a HEEL CLICK in the DRAWFRONTS. Hint: Turn out your legs for an effortless HEEL CLICK.

- **Cincinnati Variation #1** – Add a HEEL before the STEP of your TRIPLE.
  (a1e&a2)

- **Cincinnati Variation #2** – Sometimes referred to as a "Triple Cincinnati" but this term is not consistent with the traditional definition of TRIPLE. To create, simply add a BACK/HEEL and BRUSH/HEEL before you execute the TRIPLE DRAWBACK, swinging your full leg from back to front.
  (a1a2a3&a4)

- **Heel/Toe Replacements** – Replace the HEEL with TOE.

- **Shifts** – Start the DRAWBACK with the STEP or HEEL.

Maxi's & Graboffs

As noted in the Reference I section of this guidebook, the MAXI (named for the tap artist who created it: Max Ford) and the GRABOFF are kissing cousins. The basic execution of the MAXI is SHUFFLE/ LEAP/PUNCH and the breakdown of the GRABOFF is SHUFFLE/ LEAP/STEP (actually a "flying" SHUFFLE B/C). Both basics travel in the direction of the SHUFFLE and finish crossed (either front or back) of the weight-bearing leg. *

* Guidebook Note: The GRABOFF was very popular with Mr. Gene Kelly and he loved to finish each side crossed back!

- MAXI – SHUFFLE/LEAP/PUNCH
  (a1a2)

- GRABOFF – SHUFFLE/LEAP/STEP
  (a1a2)

Variations

- **Maxi w/Preparation** – Add a SINGLE, DOUBLE or TRIPLE before the SHUFFLE for a SINGLE, DOUBLE or TRIPLE MAXI. This also has a different "feel" of rhythm with the following examples of rhythmic possibilities.

Single: (1a2a3)
Double: (a1a2a3)
Triple: (&a1a2a3)

- **Graboff w/Preparation** – Use the same variations listed for MAXI w/Preparation.

- **Maxi & Graboff Combo** – The MAXI doesn't change weight, but the GRABOFF does. Try creating an 8 BAR phrase utilizing these two figures together in their simple form and then on their variations.

- **Maxi's & Graboffs w/Pickup Changes** – Add a "grace note" BRUSH within the execution of the LEAP. (*See Pullbacks, Pickups & Wings.*) These are referred to as "traditional" Graboffs or Maxi Fords.

  Example: Single Maxi w/Pickup Change:
  SHUFFLE/PICKUP CHANGE/PUNCH
  (a1&a2)

- **S/D/T/Q/Q Maxi's & Graboffs** – Create a challenge by mixing SINGLES, DOUBLES, TRIPLES, etc. with all weight changes.

  Example: A "DOUBLE/DOUBLE Maxi w/Preparation"
  DOUBLE/SHUFFLE/PICKUPCHANGE(as DOUBLE)/
  PUNCH
  (a1&a2&a)

- **Maxi's & Graboff Turns** – An en de dan (inside) turn utilizing the Maxi or Graboff with a preparation of a SINGLE/DOUBLE/TRIPLE and so on. The Maxi continues on the same preparation leg. The Graboff turn will change sides.

Bombershays

This basic is named (by some unknown source) after the French phrase "bon marché" meaning "good walk." The execution of the basic BOMBERSHAY travels toward its first sound with the action staying close to the floor. This step is usually done in succession of two or more repetitions, but is a wonderful accent step within a phrase. This was actually one of Fred Astaire's favorite basics. *

SINGLE BOMBERSHAY: STEP/BACK/HEEL STEP.

(&a1)   or   (1&a)

*Guidebook Note: Some dancers refer to the BOMBERSHAY as a sideways traveling SINGLE/DOUBLE or DOUBLE/DOUBLE. This guidebook version denotes a unique basic figure when utilizing the HEEL STAND.

Variations

- **DOUBLE Bombershay** – Replace the SINGLE or STEP with a DOUBLE.

- **TRIPLE Bombershay** – Replace the DOUBLE with a TRIPLE or maybe a QUADRUPLE.

- **Add-a-Drop** – Try adding a TOE DROP after the HEEL STAND.

- **Add-a-Heel** – As a HEEL or HEEL DROP and perhaps **Double-Up**.

- **Suzie Q** – A BOMBERSHAY that resembles a winding action of "grinding" your heel into the floor and was traditionally used as an exit step. The action is a BACK and HEEL STEP crossing over the supporting leg and traveling with the STEP to the side while rotating the weight-bearing heel out. *

  Another Suzie Q variation is BACK/STEP/HEEL/STEP. (1e&a) This version would be a DOUBLE/SINGLE BOMBERSHAY.

- **Cross Backs** – Cross the action to the back of the supporting leg.

- **Pickup & Wing Add-Ons** – After you've accomplished these moves add 'em to a BOMBERSHAY or any of the basics!

* Guidebook Note: This step was traditionally (according to Mr. "Honi" Coles) a series of flatfooted steps that actually "slid" across the floor. Its closest variation while remaining true to the rhythm is BRUSH/STOMP/STEP, with the stomping foot rocking up onto the heel in preparation for the next execution.

The Paddle & Roll

This term actually makes reference to a style of tap dance that executes close footwork with the heels and toes and is one of Mr. Bunny Brigg's favorites. The style's most common ingredient has become known as the PADDLE & ROLL (also known as a "Paradiddle") and is usually done in succession. With his famous Hoofer's "Ho-ho" track routine the "King of the Paddle & Roll" was the wonderful Mr. Lon Chaney. The SINGLE PADDLE & ROLL is:

DIG/BACK/STEP/HEEL
(1&2&)

It is common also for rhythm tap dancers to execute the following shifted pattern for a more grounded and accented feel:

HEEL/DIG/BACK/STEP
(1&2&)

Variations

- **Riff Paddles** – Add a BRUSH or TOUCH in front of the DIG for five sounds on each foot. *

* Guidebook Note: You can also think of this as an OPEN THIRD/ROLL.

- **"Double" Paddles** – Two PADDLES instead of one. **(1&2&3&)**

- **"Triple" Paddles** – Three PADDLES instead of two. **(1&2&3&4&)**

- **DOUBLE Paddle & Roll** – Replace the SINGLE weight shift with a DOUBLE. This pattern will create a rolling rhythm that shifts the accent from one sound to another. This pattern will take 20 executions (5 sounds x 4 counts) to roll over and start again on count **1**.

  (1&2&3)   *if continuing* – **(&4&1&** . . .**)**

- **TRIPLE Paddle & Roll** – Replace the DOUBLE with a TRIPLE.

- **QUADRUPLE & QUINTUPLET Paddle & Roll** – Adjust the weight change to reflect the added sounds.

- **Six Point Paddle & Poll** – This is another favorite step of mine and actually not really a Paddle & Roll. I use this close floor work figure like a Paddle & Roll — thus its name. *
  DIG/BACK/TOE/STEP/HEEL/TOE

* Guidebook Note: One of my first "Acia steps" made up many years ago, but this is actually one of Savion Glover's favorite figures! (I wish I could say I taught it to him! — Perhaps Mr. Chaney was responsible?)

- **Cross Paddle** – CHUG/BACK/STEP/HEEL/PADDLE & ROLL with the PADDLE & ROLL crossing behind the other leg.

- **Get Rid of the Heels** – This is actually a favorite step of mine to syncopate, but I haven't given it a name! (DIG/BACK/STEP in succession.)

- **Mixing Shuffles & Thirds** – Replace a few of the PADDLES with SHUFFLES or THIRDS or RIFF PADDLES to feel the difference in the close floor work and changing tones of the movement.

- **Rhythm Changes** – As with other basic variations, this is an excellent way to discover the hidden mysteries and possibilities of the PADDLE & ROLL. Utilize melody, double-time, duple or triplet time and rests to create an exciting pattern within the same figure.

- **Accent Changes** – Try accenting different sounds of the PADDLE & ROLL while keeping the basic rhythm pattern the same. This will create a wonderful series of syncopations within the even structure.

Cramp Rolls

A basic CRAMP ROLL is a step utilizing four sounds on one count with STEPS and HEELS as the basic components. Most likely an invention of Mr. John Bubbles who was first to bring heel work into tap dancing. *

* **Guidebook Note: According to "Honi" Coles, this addition of heel work in the tap dancer's repertoire was the initiation of the Bebop music trend!**

- **The Basic Cramp** – JUMP/HEEL on both feet simultaneously. JUMP equally off of both feet to straighten your relaxed legs and land in plié (with bent knees).

  (a1)

- **The Basic Cramp Roll** – With the same relaxed action of the above simple version, you will now execute two STEPS and two HEELS for 4 total sounds. Hint: relax and let the foot that will execute the first STEP hang closer to the floor. If you concentrate on separating the STEPS clearly, gravity will most often take care of the rest. Even though the first two sounds are notated as STEPS the weight should be balanced and equal over both feet during and at the conclusion of the figure. *

STEP/STEP/HEEL/HEEL
(e&a1) - R L R L or L R L R

* **Guidebook Note: This basic can also be executed slowly and without the jumping action for rhythmic purpose, phrasing and breaking the figure down for practice.**

Variations

- **Cheater's Cramp Roll** – ROLL (no/weight)/HEEL in the action of a B/C.
  (&a1)

- **Press Cramp Roll** – HEEL/ROLL (no weight)/HEEL with the action of a B/C. (e&a1)

- **Reverse Cramp Roll** – Sometimes called an "Around the World." This Cramp Roll reverses the order of the HEELS; i.e. instead of R L R L execute R L L R. The action is benefited by starting with an extended leg to your 1:00 position *(see Warmup)*. Take your first sound as a LEAP and fully shift (and keep) your weight to finish with a B/C action.

LEAP/TOUCH/HEEL DROP/HEEL.

- **Heel Cramp Roll** – Same as the basic or reverse but beginning on HEEL STEPS and ending with TOES. Note: Be careful to time your landing with a good plié, otherwise you'll feel quite a jolt!

- **Crawling Cramp Roll** – Like CRAWLS, but utilizing both feet and in the order of a CRAMP ROLL. These can travel in any direction.

- **Jimmy Crawl** – A Jimmy Slyde step that starts a Crawling Heel Cramp Roll with a STEP.

- **S/D/T/Q/Q Cramp Rolls** – Replace the initial STEP with a DOUBLE, TRIPLE, QUADRUPLE, etc. You can also do the same for the second STEP.

The Ad-Lib

The Ad-Lib is based on a simple figure by the late Eddie Brown that resembles a Paddle & Roll but involves additional heel action. This figure can be executed in place or traveling and has one weight change per execution.

- **SINGLE Ad-Lib** – DIG/BACK/HEEL/STEP B/C (WITH HEELS).
  (1&a2&a)

- **DOUBLE Ad-Lib** – Replace the STEP (or SINGLE) with a DOUBLE.
  (1&a2&a3)

- **TRIPLE Ad-Lib** – Replace the DOUBLE with a TRIPLE. (1&2&3&4&)

- **QUADRUPLE Ad-Lib** – Replace the TRIPLE with a QUA-DRUPLE. (1&2&3&4&1)

- **QUINTUPLET Ad-Lib** – Replace the QUADRUPLE with a QUINTUPLET. (1&2&3&4&1&)

Variations

- **Toe Punch Add-On** – Insert a PUNCH and HEEL before executing the SINGLE, DOUBLE, TRIPLE and so on in your Ad-Lib.

  Example: DOUBLE TOE PUNCH ADD-ON AD-LIB (1&2&3&4&1)

- **Continuations** – Run the Ad-Lib's consecutively.

- **Rhythm Changes** – Syncopation works well with this figure (after practicing in even fashion) as well as triplets. Also, try again with a common melody.

- **Double-Up** – Try repeating each individual sound twice!

- **Home Base** – Start with an Ad-Lib and create other rhythmic figures and return back to the Ad-Lib as "home base."

Pullbacks, Pickups & Wings

These basic "air steps" are executed with relaxed and straight legs utilizing the principals outlined in the Warm-up section and are motivated by one of the Creation Five: The *"Pull."*

All of these steps require the dancer to leave the floor in order to execute the first sound, whether a BRUSH, a BACK or a SCRAPE. For PULLBACKS & PICKUPS, the dancer travels to the back and for the WING, the dancer stays neutral.

Pullbacks & Pickups

The Basic Pullback is a modified JUMP with two DOUBLES (BACK) executed on both feet simultaneously. The terminology for this basic changes from region to region even across the U.S. (i.e. "Pullback" is used for any airborne BRUSH STEP executed from two weight bearing legs. The most difficult action to master is the JUMP action of leaving the floor in order to execute the BACK. *

* Guidebook Note: These actions can be practiced holding onto a ballet barre or chair if needed. However, many students are able to execute the basic PULL-BACK, PICKUP or WING without this. Remember that BACK is the notation for Back Brush.

Exercise #8 – Stand in neutral with your weight balanced on both feet. Plié (bend your knees) and JUMP up and back about a foot in distance landing on the balls of your feet. Remember that your hips are the motivation; the *"Pull"* and *"Fall"* actions are your core movements and straight, relaxed legs is your goal. A BACK inserted within the JUMP will create your basic PULLBACK. (a1)

- **Pickup** – The same action as the PULLBACK but on one foot as in a modified HOP. A BACK/STEP on a weight bearing leg.

- **Pickup Change** – A modified LEAP with a BACK. Same as PICKUP but changing your HOP to a LEAP.

Variations

- **Pickover** – Same as PICKUP but with a BRUSH to travel front.

- **Pullover** – Same as PULLBACK but with a BRUSH.

- **Pullsides** & **Picksides** – Same as the above but traveling sideways and actually BRUSHING to the side of your feet. *

* Guidebook Note: It's easier to travel in the opposite direction of your first action foot. For instance, if you're creating a PULLSIDE starting with the right foot you will find it easier to travel to the left.

- **Four Sound Pullback Variation** – Most common execution involves BACK/BACK/STEP/STEP (RLRL or LRLR). You can also execute a PULLOVER with BRUSH/BRUSH/STEP/STEP. *

* Guidebook Note: Be aware that this step is in the same foot order as a PULL-BACK a close (and confusing) relative is the Double FLAP (two FLAPS or DOUBLES executed back to back).

- **Three Sound Pick Variation** – Execute an extra BRUSH (on the same leg) while airborne during a PICKUP or PICKOVER.

- **Toe Punch Add-On** – Try adding a PUNCH after the BRUSH or BACK before you land.

- **S/D/T/Q/Q** – Change your weight with any of these instead of SINGLES!

Wings

This basic is actually a modified SHUFFLE STEP or TRIPLE on both feet simultaneously. It is a completely different step than the PULLBACK or PICKUP but requires the same preparation and relaxation. In this case, your core movements are *"Throw," "Pull"* and *"Fall,"* and the movement is a modified JUMP.

Exercise #9 - Stand neutral with your weight balanced on both feet. Now, shift your weight to your left leg while executing a SHUFFLE/TOUCH with your right leg. Now, the difference with this move and the standard TRIPLE (other than the absence of a weight change) is that the first sound will actually SCRAPE off the side of your foot to create the unique first WING sound. * Remember again that your foot and knee are totally relaxed. For clarification, you can define this action with SLIDE/BACK/TOUCH — *"Throw," "Pull" and "Drop"*.

(&a1) - *repeat for 8 counts and then reverse sides.*

* Guidebook Note: This exercise will help you feel the TRIPLE action while finishing in the initial neutral position.

When you're ready for both feet, JUMP off the floor as you execute your WING as a TRIPLE on both feet, finding the correct "timing" for your body and the creation of three distinct sounds. Remember to straighten your relaxed legs for the SHUFFLE action.

- **Single Wing** – The same as a Basic WING but on one foot. A modified HOP.

- **Swap** – A SINGLE WING changing the HOP to a LEAP.

Variations

- **"Double" Wing** – A 6 sound WING that is divided by its sides with the left or right foot initiating the first sound followed by the other side: R L R L R L.

  SCRAPE/SCRAPE/BACK/BACK/STEP/STEP.
  (a4e&a1) or all 6 sounds "on top of" count 1

- **Five Sound Wing #1** – Replace the STEPS (or SINGLES) with DOUBLES or PUNCH/STEPS.

- **Five Sound Wing #2 (Basic Condos Wing)** – Utilizes QUINTUPLETS ("Double" SHUFFLE/STEP) in place of the standard TRIPLES. *

* Guidebook Note: This incredible step was created by Frank Condos of the Condos Brothers, but he would execute the step as a SWAP by replacing the STEP with a LEAP.

- **Toe Stand Wing** – Any WING variation executed on the tip of your toe rather than the ball of your foot.

- **Pendulum Wing** – Execute a BRUSH before the SINGLE WING and a BACK afterward in the action of a pendulum.

- **Saw Wing** – Execute the Single WING with a PUNCH behind and/or in front of the supporting leg. A bent elbow action of the non-weight-bearing side of the body (as if sawing a log) gives this step its name.

Thirds

This figure is a modified SHUFFLE or DOUBLE with a HEEL TAP, DIG or TOE TAP sandwiched in the middle that is created either as "closed" or "open." The basic core action is *"Throw."*

- **Open Third** – Sometimes called a "riffle" (but not in this guidebook — that's something else!) While executing a SHUFFLE, you relax your foot closer to the floor to add a HEEL TAP between the two SHUFFLE sounds. This figure can be created slow or on one count. *

* **Guidebook Note: A slow closed THIRD would be a basic 3-point CRAWL without crawling.**

- **Closed Third** – Sometimes called a "flat FLAP" or "Slurp." This has the extra DIG between the BRUSH and STEP of a DOUBLE. This can also be done with a SLAP for no weight change.

- **Open Toe Third** – A wonderful little "word" that was handed down to me by Fred Moritel and made famous by Sam Weber.

This action is a straight leg SHUFFLE variation that adds an extra toe tap for three sounds. To create, you start with your leg *"Lifted"* to the side of your body ("turned-out" from the hip) and extend your SHUFFLE action (*"Throw"*) to a straight "turned-in" leg under your body. * Try adding a BACK for four sounds too!

* **Guidebook Note: This is easier to find if you aim the outside of your working leg's foot toward the floor. You can also reverse the action and start in front of your body "turned-in" and finish "turned-out."**

- **Closed Toe Third** – Replace the SHUFFLE with a DOUBLE to finish with a change of weight.

- **"Double" Open Third** – Two Thirds instead of one; a nice variation with Paddles.

- **Inserts** – Utilize Thirds with Paddle & Rolls, Ad-Libs, Maxi's, Pickups etc.

- **Add-Ons** – Add PUNCHES, HEELS, TOES to the end of Thirds of any kind.

Essence & Waltz Clog

These two basics are actually two distinct styles and origins of tap dance but for this guidebook will be introduced as the same basic figure. The Essence is a leftover step from an old dance called *The Virginia Essence* and is now often referred to as *The Old Softshoe*. Both the Essence and The Waltz Clog share common footwork with the biggest difference being the Time Signature. The Essence is danced in 4/4 time while the Waltz Clog (as its name implies) is danced in 3/4. The terms SINGLE, DOUBLE, TRIPLE, QUADRUPLE and QUINTU-PLET are the variation tools of the basic figure.

All of the basic patterns listed below (excluding the variations) are SINGLE B/C's or SINGLE/SINGLE/STEP.

- **Basic Front Essence** – This figure is simply a STEP B/C, with the B/C crossing in front of the supporting leg from side to side. (1a2 3a4)

- **Back Essence** – Same as above but crossing to the back. *

* **Guidebook Note: The Traditional "Back Essence" is my "Cross Back Essence" listed below. The change of term is relative to the execution of the exact opposite of the "Front Essence."**

- **Cross Back Essence** – The first STEP is behind your support-ing leg with the B/C being to the side to finish under your body.

- **Cross Front Essence** – Same as above but crossing in front of the supporting leg. Same as a Cross B/C in Jazz dance.

- **Front Crossing Essence** – Step, B/C, B/C, B/C crossing the first   B/C to the front of the supporting leg (crossed) and then open to the side and return on the third B/C to crossing front.

- **Back Crossing Essence** – Same as the above but crossing in back of the supporting leg.

Essence Turn (The Paddle Turn)

This turn is the most common turn involved with Essence combinations and steps.

- **The Basic Paddle Turn** – STEP, B/C, B/C, B/C turning in an en dehors or en dedan fashion (i.e. "inside" toward the supporting leg or "outside" away from the supporting leg).

Essence Variations

- **S/D/T/Q/Q** – Simply change the SINGLE/SINGLE basics listed above to DOUBLE/DOUBLES, SINGLE/TRIPLES etc. keeping the "essence" of the figure's basic rhythm.

Example #1: DOUBLE, DOUBLE FRONT ESSENCE (a1&a2 a3&a4) – Right & Left

Example #2: DOUBLE, DOUBLE FRONT CROSSING (a1&a2&a3&a4) – Right

Example #3: DOUBLE, DOUBLE PADDLE TURN (a1&a2&a3&a4) – Left

Example #4: DOUBLE, TRIPLE, BACK ESSENCE (a1e&a2) – Right

DOUBLE, DOUBLE FRONT ESSENCE (a3&a4) – Left

Dance all of the above examples in sequence and repeat on the other side and you've created an Essence Step (8 Bars)!

- **Heel Add-Ons** – Try adding HEEL and HEEL DROP work to the basic Essence figures.

- **"Pursuit"** – This Essence variation figure shows an example of basic figure creation technique.

HEEL/SHUFFLE/TOUCH B/C (HEELS)/BACK/STEP (2x)
(1e&a 2e&a 3e&a 4e&a)

- **Traveling Essence** – Move the figure front, back, turning, etc.

- **Rhythm Changes** – The Essence figure is one of the most versatile basics in tap dance to play with rhythmically.

- **Inserts** – Try inserting other basics for new figures!

The Waltz Clog

The basic Waltz Clog is a SINGLE/TRIPLE/BACK ESSENCE in 3/4 time.

(1a2a3 1a2a3) – to complete both sides

- **Common Waltz Clog** – The version most of us will do upon request is a DOUBLE/TRIPLE/BACK ESSENCE in 3/4 time. (a1a2a3 a1a2a3)

Variations

- **S/D/T/Q/Q** – Same as the Essence Variations but in 3/4 Waltz Time.

- **Polyrhythms** – Try the Waltz Clog in any form with its 3/4 structure using a tune in 4/4. *

(DOUBLE - dbl, SHUFFLE - s, B/C - b/c)

1	2	3	4	1	2	3	4
a1	a2	a3	a1	a2	a3	a1	a2
dbl	s	b/c	dbl	s	b/c	dbl	s

* **Guidebook Note: Anita Feldman is a tap master of polyrhythms. Her book** *Inside Tap* **covers numerous multi-rhythm combinations and exercises.** *(See Appendix.)*

Turns

Basic turns utilized in ballet, jazz and modern dance are the foundation of most tap turns. These basic turns include: chainé, pencil, 3-step, pirouette, pivot, skater's, barrel, axle and paddle turn (covered in this chapter under *The Essence & Waltz Clog*) among others. For basic execution of these dance basics seek a respectable dance educator in your area. All tap footwork can be utilized within these structures.

If you are familiar with these terms, here are a few examples of common tap turns.

- **Chainés** – Utilize SINGLES, DOUBLES, TRIPLES etc. and RIFFS as en dedans (inside) or en dehors (outside) turns. Even and syncopated rhythm combinations are endless. HEEL Add-Ons are also a great way to use this basic turn.

- **Pirouette** – This simple turn can be utilized within any tap choreography with added sounds both on the outside and the supporting leg. A fun variation is with the STOMP or Buck Time Step *(see next chapter)*.

- **Cramp Roll Turn** – This basic tap turn is an en dedans turn traditionally utilizing a STAMP and DOUBLE CRAMP ROLL. (1a2&a3)

- **Basic Maxi Turn** – An en dedans turn utilizing a STEP and SINGLE MAXI. (1a2a3)

- **Rhythm Turn** – An en dedans turn utilizing the "Jimmy Crawl" *(see Cramp Rolls)* and often beginning with a SHUFFLE, "Pendulum Wing" *(see Wings)* or BACK/STEP.

Variations

Turns are an endless world of possibilities. Good basic understanding of this basic dance component will open up many opportunities for turns with any tap figure.

Thoughts. . .

Well, did you make it through all of that? If so, I hope the ideas will perpetuate for many years and that you came up with many new creations! As mentioned previously, many of the listed variations will cross over into all other steps, figures and combinations in this guidebook; the divisions by which I show example are by no means all of the possibilities!

Now, with a foundation of basics, let's go on to some traditional and not-so-traditional phrases and choruses in Chapters Three and Four as . . .

your rhythmic journey continues.

Chapter Three

Traditional &
Not-So-Traditional
Time Steps

Play

Time Steps

The following is a collection of "time steps." This eight BAR structure originated as a means of setting up tempo and style for a tap dancer's band as an a capella introduction by the dancer. A two BAR pattern was traditionally repeated three times (straight or in variations) and followed by a "break" to lead in for the musicians. The most famous is the . . .

Stomp Time Step ("Buck" Time Step)

Often referred to as *"the* time step," variations of this simple figure are utilized in all styles and forms of tap. The most common variations include the SINGLE, DOUBLE and TRIPLE Stomp Timesteps. For this guidebook, however, I will dissect this step even further to define these as SINGLE/DOUBLE, DOUBLE/DOUBLE and TRIPLE/DOUBLE. *

* Guidebook Note: Some teachers utilize an old phrase to teach the rhythm of this basic Time Step: "Thanks *for* the buggy ride" for the SINGLE/DOUBLE, "Thank *you for* the buggy ride" for the DOUBLE/DOUBLE, and "When *'ll we take* a buggy ride" for the TRIPLE/DOUBLE. I actually avoid utilizing this ditty in that the step actually starts on count 4 as a musical pickup and ends on count 3, unlike the singing phrase which starts on count 1 and ends on 4. For intermediate dancers, it's no big deal and a great way to remember, but it will drive a beginner crazy!

The swinging eighth note or triplet feel will bring you closer to the traditional timing which "pushes" the off-beats closer to their following eighth note by utilizing "a" instead of "&" (4123a4123a). A beginner, however will greatly benefit from practicing in straight eighth note time (duple feel) utilizing the "&" rather than "a".

This basic can also be executed as a **Standard Time Step** by replacing the STOMP with a SHUFFLE (starting on 4& or 4a). I introduce the STOMP version first to emphasize the importance of a relaxed leg and ankle and the necessary action of lifting the leg from the hip.

- **SINGLE/SINGLE Stomp Time Step Basic**
  STOMP/HOP/STEP B/C (STEP/STEP front to back). *
  (*repeat*)
  (4123a 4123a)   or   (4123& 4123&)

* Guidebook Note: Remember that a B/C (BALL CHANGE) is not a complete change of weight; it's just enough to get your other foot off the floor.

- **SINGLE/DOUBLE Stomp Time Step**
  Traditional "Single"
  Replace the second STEP (the first SINGLE within the B/C) with a DOUBLE.   (*repeat*)
  (412a3a 412a3a)   or   (412&3& 412&3&)

- **DOUBLE/DOUBLE Stomp Time Step**
  Traditional "Double"
  Replace the first STEP (SINGLE) with a DOUBLE. (*repeat*)
  (41a2a3a 41a2a3a)   or   (41&2&3& 41&2&3&)

- **TRIPLE/DOUBLE Stomp Time Step**
  Traditional "Triple"
  Replace the first STEP (SINGLE) with a TRIPLE. (*repeat*)
  (41&a2a3a41&a2a3a)   or   (41&a2&3& 41&a2&3&)

- **TRIPLE/TRIPLE Stomp Time Step**
  Traditional "Double-Triple"
  Replace the second DOUBLE with a TRIPLE. *(repeat)*
  (41&a2&a3a41&a2&a3a)   or   (41&a2&a3& 41&a2&a3&)

- **Jackie Gleason Break** - Dance one BAR of the TRIPLE/
  TRIPLE Stomp Time Step and attach a DOUBLE IRISH B/C
  (SHUFFLE/HOP/BRUSH/STEP B/C). *
  (41&a2&a3a4a1a2a3)   or   (41&a2&a3&4&1&2&3)

* Guidebook Note: The TRIPLE/TRIPLE Jackie Gleason Break is actually my
name for this common and traditional break. Find some footage of Mr. Gleason
and you'll find why I gave this step his name! "And away we go..."

Variations

- **S/D/T/Q/Q** – Change the basic weight change to TRIPLES,
  QUADRUPLES, etc.

- **Hop Time Variation** – Add additional HOPS to each variation. Two HOPS for a DOUBLE/DOUBLE or three for a
  TRIPLE/DOUBLE.

- **Add-a-Heel** – Add HEELS to SINGLE, DOUBLES,
  TRIPLES, HOPS, etc. Try multiple HEELS and B/C's with
  HEELS.

- **Cramp Rolls, Crawls and Riff Variations** – Where can you
  fit any of these figures in without losing the rhythmic integrity
  of the step? Or, for that matter, try changing the rhythm completely! Thousands of new Timesteps have been created with
  this basic variation technique!

- **Leap Time** – Change the HOP to a LEAP.

- **Turn Variations** – HOPS are an easy place to turn . . . anywhere else?

- **Basic Start Variations** – Change the STOMP to a SHUFFLE, SCUFFLE, PADDLE, BACK, etc. Don't feel obligated to always start on count 4, but do keep the integrity of the HOP on count one if you want the traditional feel.

- **Hop Variations** – Change the HOP to a PICKUP, PICKOVER, Single WING or SWAP.

- **Punch Add-Ons** – Insert PUNCHES and HEELS.

- **Rhythm Changes** – Play with this traditional figure in not-so-traditional rhythms.

Traveling Time Step

This traditional figure is also known as a SINGLE, DOUBLE or TRIPLE and the breaks differ from one dancer to another. I utilize a simple vocal "ditty" to teach this rhythm pattern that's notated below with a straight eighth note feel. With the exception of the break, this figure travels side to side in the direction of the first SHUFFLE.

- **SINGLE Traveling Time Step**
  "Every cup of coffee I consume, I need a donut".
  4& **1** & 2& **3** &4 **1** 2 & **3**&
  SHUFFLE/STEP/SHUFFLE B/C B/C HOP/*STEP*/SHUFFLE STEP

- **DOUBLE Traveling Time Step**
  "Every cup of coffee I consume, yes I need a donut".
  4 & **1** & 2 & **3** & 4 **1** & 2 & **3** &
  Replace the *STEP* (SINGLE) with a DOUBLE.

- **TRIPLE Traveling Time Step**
  "Every cup of coffee I consume, I really need a donut".
  4 & **1** & 2 & **3** & 4 **1** & a 2 & **3** &
  Replace the DOUBLE with a TRIPLE.

- **Continuation Traveling Break**
  "And a cup of sugar in the pot will make it taste just fine right now".
  4 & **1** & 2 & **3** & 4 & **1** & 2 & **3** & 4
  (SHUFFLE/STEP) x ,4/IRISH/CLAP

- **Traditional Traveling Break**
  "And a cup of sweet sugar in the pot will make it great!"
  4 & **1** 2 & **3** & 4 & **1** & 2 & **3**
  SHUFFLE/HOP/HOP/DOUBLE/STEP/SHUFFLE/HOP/
  DOUBLE/STEP/STAMP

Variations

- **Swing It!** – Change your duple time to a triple time "feel."

- **Silence Is Golden** – Where can you insert that perfect silence for at least a full BEAT?

- **Heel Add-Ons** – Add HEELS to weight changes *and* non-weight changes with DROPS or SCUFFS.

- **Turn Variations** – Add a pirouette to the HOP or try a chainé to travel.

- **Slide Variations** – Add SLIDES or CHUGS to weight shifts.

- **Rhythm Changes** – Again, one of the best ways to discover a new idea!

- **Splits** – Take part of the figure and add another such as 1/2 of the DOUBLE Traveling Time (1 BAR) and 1/2 of the TRIPLE/ TRIPLE Stomp Time.

- **Inserts** – Where will a basic pattern or variation fit? Try a PADDLE & ROLL, a DRAWBACK . . .

- **Double-Up**, **Melody** or **Accent Variations** – Utilize any and all of the previously listed variations throughout the guidebook!

Rhythm Time

This basic foundation step was a favorite of the late Leon Collins (not necessarily by this name!) as well as his living legacy, Ms. Dianne Walker. A relative by variation is The Manhattan Time Step *(see Variations)*.

- **The Basic Rhythm Time Step**
  (CHUG) X 4 /CLAP/DOUBLE/DOUBLE/TRIPLE/TRIPLE
  (a4a1&(2)a3a4a1a2a3) *(repeat 3X)* *

* Guidebook Note: I refer to this basic as a DOUBLE/DOUBLE/TRIPLE TRIPLE Rhythm Time Step with the DOUBLE executed with a BACK. Try a SINGLE/ TRIPLE/DOUBLE/TRIPLE!

Variations

- **Basic Rhythm Break**
  (CHUG) X 4/DOUBLE/DOUBLE/CHUG/CHUG/DOUBLE DOUBLE/STAMP/STAMP
  (a4a1a2a3a4a1a2a3)

- **S/D/T/Q/Q** – Variations on the weight changes!

- **Heel Add-Ons** – Add those HEELS to the different weight changes as well as accents!

- **Step Variations** – Change the STEPS to HOPS or LEAPS.

- **Stop When They Least Expect It** – Try that silence . . . in surprising places.

- **Manhattan Time Step** – Basic traditional formula for many new variations!
  (CHUG) x4 / STEP/ STEP/SHUFFLE/HOP/STEP/STEP *
  (a4a1&(2)&(3)4a123)

* Guidebook Note: This step is mostly used in variation by switching the first STEP to a DOUBLE, the second STEP to a TRIPLE and the final two STEPS to DOUBLES without losing the skeleton or basic rhythmic figure.

- **Rhythm Changes**, **Hop Variations** and more!

Swing Time

This SHUFFLE B/C figure is a wonderful basic open to many exciting possibilities. A master of this figure and its many variations is Ms. Sarah Petronio.

- **Basic Swing Time**
  SHUFFLE B/C /DOUBLE/SHUFFLE B/C /DOUBLE/
  DOUBLE/STEP
  (1&a2a3a4a1a2a3a)

  SHUFFLE B/C /DOUBLE/SHUFFLE B/C /DOUBLE/STEP
  (1&a2a3a4a1a2a(**3**))

Variations & Breaks

By now, you should be getting the idea! Just remember a Time Step is an 8 BAR Phrase that repeats a 2 BAR figure 3 times (either identically or in variation) and is followed by a 2 BAR break! Try "Swing Time" with its traditional repetition and add your own break. *

* Guidebook Note: Some teachers break down the time step phrase into 6 steps and a two BAR break. I have kept the 2 BAR step definition based on music structure as well as the commonality of all time steps.

Acia's Traveling Time Step #1

The following is a fun Time Step basic utilizing STOMPS and STAMPS! *

HEEL/STOMP/STAMP
(a12)

BACK/STEP/STOMP/BACK/*STEP/STAMP/STEP/STAMP*
(a3a4a1a2)

BACK/STEP/STOMP/BACK/*STEP/STAMP*/CHUG/CHUG
(a3a4a1 2 3)

SLAM w/weight /BACK/STEP/STOMP/BACK *STEP/
STAMP*
(4a1a2a3)

* Guidebook Note: This complete four BAR figure has many BALL CHANGES, all noted in italics.

Variations

Make up your own two variations and send me a great new break!

One Potato

This is a simple PADDLE & ROLL Time Step that I made up with endless variation possibilities. Here's another "ditty" to remember the figure and the simple sixteenth note rhythm:

(1e&a 2e&a 3e&a ....)

"One potato, two potato, three potato, four potato, chives and butter and some salt and pepper and a Coca-Cola" (That's Margarita if you're over 18!)

The "One Potato" 2 BAR figure repeats R L R before the break.

- **One Potato** – Simple PADDLE & ROLL series starting with the HEEL and ending with the STEP.
  (1e&a2e&a3e&a4e&a)

  HEEL/B/C (HEELS)/DIG/BACK/STEP (2x) *
  (1e&a2e&a3e&a)

  HEEL/DIG/BACK/STEP (PADDLE & ROLL starting with the HEEL).
  (4e&a)

* Guidebook Note: Remember a BALL CHANGE (B/C) always ends on the weight-bearing leg!

Variations & Breaks

- **One Potato Break** – A continuation of the sixteenth note feel with the triple HEEL/PADDLE & ROLL variation listed above and a SHUFFLE/Heel Toe Clip/STEP/Toe-Heel Clip/STAMP figure to close on count 4 of the eighth BAR. *

* Guidebook Note: If you figured that one out, you're doin' great and you're tuning up your tools of creation!

Hip Hop Time

This is one of my favorite basic Timesteps. I created it sometime in the 80's but have changed the name to reflect the times. This is also, like "One Potato," a sixteenth note continuation with HEEL accents. This figure repeats R L R before the Break.

BACK/HEEL/TRIPLE w-HEEL/"Double" PADDLE & ROLL
(2x)
(a1e&a2e&a3e&a4e&a1)

SHUFFLE/HEEL/PADDLE & ROLL/DIG/BACK HEEL/
FLAP
(e&a2e&a3e&a4)

- **The Hip Hop Time Break**
  BACK/CHUG/SHUFFLE/CHUG/SHUFFLE/STEP * (3x)
  (a1e&a2e&a3e&a4 e&a1e&a2e&)

  BACK/HEEL/SHUFFLE/PUNCH/CLAP
  (a3e&a4)

* Guidebook Note: This is a simple TRIPLE Drawback (or Cincinnati) variation.

Variations

- **S/D/T/Q/Q** – In this case, try replacing the TRIPLES with QUADRUPLES or QUINTUPLETS.

- **Rhythm Shift** – Try this figure with triplets instead of sixteenth notes and make adjustments to fit the Time Step structure.

Chapter Four

Traditional Choruses

Structure

The Shim Sham Shimmy

This simple Time Step chorus has been lovingly referred to as "the tap dance anthem" for its timelessness and universal rhythmic appeal. The original collection of figures by Leonard Reed was based on popular and vernacular dances of the late 1920's. The following two versions are in simple (#1) and traditional (#2) forms. "The Shim Sham," however, has been done in many different "accents" and "styles" depending on the lineage of dancers it's connected to. The simple (#1) is close to a Henry LeTang beginner's version and the traditional (#2) is most often used as a universal tap dance encore and based on Mr. Reed's original. * This chorus traditionally starts on the right leg.

* **Guidebook Note: For reference information on Leonard Reed and The Shim Sham Shimmy (*see Appendix*).**

Shim Sham Shimmy #1 *(Basic)*

(This version has the same break to complete every Time Step.)

- **The Shim Sham** (1st Step)
  TRIPLE/TRIPLE/SHUFFLE B/C (STEP/STAMP)/TRIPLE
  (4&12&34&1&2&3) — repeat 3x's changing the last sound on the final side to a TOUCH.

- **Basic Shim Sham Break**
  CLAP/STAMP/STEP/HOP/STEP/HOP/STEP/JUMP/JUMP
  (4123&(4)a123) — This break crosses front of the standing leg with the STAMP and moves back with first STEP and consecutive STEPS. The first JUMP is out (to parallel 2nd position) and the second JUMP is underneath the body with feet together (in parallel 1st). *

127

* Guidebook Note: Here's a great example that ballet and jazz dance knowledge can further define your tap creations! As promised, however, this book will not cover basic body positions of ballet and/or jazz. Too many wonderful reference books are written solely for that purpose.

- **The Cross-Step** (2nd Step)
  TOUCH/HEEL/TOUCH/HEEL/STEP/HEEL/STEP/HEEL/
  STEP
  (412341a2**3**) — *repeat 3x's changing the last sound on the final side to a TOUCH.*

  This step travels in the direction of the first TOUCH and crosses over (or front) with the second ROLL (the STEP/HEEL) and switches direction when repeating.
  Break

- **The Tack-Annie** (3rd Step)
  STAMP/(STAMP/BACK/TOUCH x 3)/STAMP/BACK/STEP
  (a4a12a3**4**a1a2a**3**) *repeat 3x's*

  The STAMPS are executed in a wide second position (wider than shoulder width) and the BACK (BRUSHES) are *"Pulled"* to meet the standing leg for the TOUCH. All movement is motivated by the hips. *
  Break

* Guidebook Note: According to the late Charles "Honi" Coles, this step was originated by paying "tribute" to a fairly overweight prostitute (Annie) in the action of showing her guest the way out of the front door . . . from the waist down. Others say *she* was being hauled off by the police!

- **The Half-Break** (4th Step)

  This step is also referred to as "Falling off a Log" but is not the truest and complete form of that step *(see Chapter Five)*. "Half-Break" refers to taking the break halfway through as well as at the end of the 8 Bars.

  STAMP/STEP/SHUFFLE B/C (2x's)

  (41a2a3 41a2a3)

  Break

  Repeat the 2 BAR "Half-Break" and the Break again to finish 8 bars. Some dancers change the last JUMP (In) to a SLIDE in on both feet.

Shim Sham Shimmy #2

(This version changes the first two steps and the break only by bringing the sounds closer to the floor).

* Guidebook Note: Remember that The Shim Sham Shimmy is a collection of Timesteps! This first step is also commonly executed with a STOMP rather than a DIG.

- **The Shim Sham** (1st Step)

  Change the TRIPLES in version #1 to DIG/BACK/STEP.

- **The Shim Sham Break #2**

  (Also completes 3rd & 4th Steps.)

  STAMP/TOUCH/ROLL/ROLL/STEP/STAMP/STAMP *

  (4123&(4)&123)

* Guidebook Note: Notice the term ROLL again is being used to simplify the notation of STEP/HEEL.

This break crosses the first STAMP in front of the standing leg, crosses the TOUCH behind and continues the crossing back movement (as does version #1) until executing the STAMP/STAMP in a narrow parallel second (approximately shoulder width under your hips).

- **The Cross-Step** (2nd Step)
  CHUG/STEP/CHUG/STEP/ROLL/ROLL/STEP
  (412341a23) 3x's

  The crossing action is the same as the #1 version.

  Cross-Step Break: ROLL/ROLL/STEP/ROLL/ROLL/TOUCH
  (412341&(2)&3)

  Continue to cross front with the second ROLL (on each side) changing directions with the STEP (as a pivot).

- **The Tack-Annie** (3rd Step)
  Same as version #1 with break #2.

- **The Half-Break** (4th Step)
  Same as version #1 with break #2.

Variations

- **Drawback Add-Ons** – Add two Drawbacks to the second BAR of Step #2 and Step #3 (The Cross-Step and Tack Annie.) *

* **Guidebook Note: You can actually see the most common Drawback variations in an available videotape entitled "Leonard Reed's Shim Sham Shimmy."** *(See Appendix — Resources & Supplies).*

- **Rhythmic Integrity** – Try keeping the same rhythmic pattern of the Shim Sham Shimmy and replace the footwork to discover a new creation!

- **Accent Changes** – Change the natural accents that occur within this traditional step. For instance, the accents of Step #1 naturally fall of the STEPS or the Downbeats of the first BAR. Try shifting the accent on each leg to a different place and perhaps to yet another the next time around!

- **Mix & Match** – Go back and use other basic steps and figures for a new Shim Sham Shimmy! A Paddle & Roll version, a Drawback version, a Pickup version, a Stomp Time Step version, a Traveling Time Step version, or an Ad-Lib version. Create new traditions!

The B.S. Chorus

Well, they say it doesn't stand for Boy Scout . . . and it's "beautiful steps" according to Bunny Briggs!

This collection of traditional favorites is a chorus (32 BARS) of well-known (and sometimes overused) figures from tap's heyday. Everyone should, in my opinion, know this one and execute it well when proficiency of basics has been proven. This B.S. Chorus version was handed down from Mr. Charles "Honi" Coles and lovingly held in tradition by Ms. Brenda Bufalino. *(See Appendix for information on Brenda*

Bufalino and Charles "Honi" Coles videotapes!) These classics are time-tested and actually were executed at "breakneck" speed This chorus, like the Shim Sham Shimmy, traditionally starts with the first sound on the right leg. *

* Guidebook Note: The fast, traditional speed greatly affects the execution of Step #3 and Step #4 which are both much more difficult at a slower tempo.

- **"The" Time Step** (Step #1)
  STOMP/BACK/HOP/DOUBLE/DOUBLE/STEP   *
  (4a1a2a3a4a1a2a3a) 3x's

* Guidebook Note: This is a traditional DOUBLE Stomp Time Step. This is my STOMP/BACK/DOUBLE/DOUBLE Time Step.

- **The B.S. Break**
  STOMP/BACK/HOP/LEAP/DIG/BACK/HOP/DOUBLE/
  MAXI W/PICKUP CHANGE/STAMP
  (4a1a2a3a4a1&a23)

- **The Cross Over** (Step #2)
  STOMP/BACK/HEEL/TRIPLE/DOUBLE(BACK)/IRISH
  (FRONT)/HEEL/SNAP *
  (4a1&a2a3a4a123) 3x's
  Break

Start your STOMP crossing your standing leg with your Cincinnati (BACK/HEEL/TRIPLE) *"Pulling"* your body and your DOUBLE towards a diagonal back. Cross your DOUBLE (also in front of your standing leg) before executing the IRISH.

* Guidebook Note: On your third repetition, replace the last SNAP with a STAMP to prepare for the break on the right leg. This SNAP can also be replaced with two DOUBLES traveling to the direction of your next side — a3&a instead of 3.

- **The Wing Step** (Step #3)
  TRIPLE/BRUSH/TRIPLE(WING)/STEP/MAXI
  w/PICK CHANGE/STAMP *
  (4a1a2a34a1&a23) 3x's
  Break

* Guidebook Note: This actually could be called the Wing Time Step but a variation of the B.S. Step #1 holds that title; just replace the last STEP (or SINGLE) with a TRIPLE. The timing makes the step appear to create a Single WING if the dancer is lifted up during the DOUBLE (4a1a2a3e&a). Hint: Keep your weight on the DOUBLE while executing the beginning of the TRIPLE. This action will enable you to SCRAPE the first sound of the TRIPLE and execute a "fake" WING.

- **Over-the-Tops** (First figure of Step #4)
  This step is actually done in halftime (or half the preceding speed) and will utilize 4 complete BARS.

  STEP/SLIDE/HOP   STEP/SLIDE/HOP
  (123(4))   (123(4))

  PUNCH/HOP/STEPSLIDE/HOP/STEP/SLIDE/HOP
  (41234 123(4))

  STEP behind your standing leg each time with your SLIDE (off the outside of your foot) going from the front of your body to the back; HOPPING eventually (with practice!) will be over your SLIDING leg that will move straight, under your HOP and end fully behind you. *

* Guidebook Note: The incredible Nicholas Brothers were famous for their rubber leg versions of this one! *(See Appendix — Resources & Supplies for information on Harold and Fayard Nicholas.)*

You should now have your weight on your left foot and if you made it through your Over-the-Top's that foot should be in front of the right! Now, as an exercise, PULL your straight left leg to the back of your body utilizing the ball of your foot and STEP. (In the first edition of this book, this basic was defined incorrectly as a SLIDE/LEAP.)

PULL/STEP
(a1)

Next: Exaggerate your STEP by *"Lifting"* your knee from the back of your body to the front letting your PULL be *"Pulled"* to the back at the same time. After you have found your "timing" and are able to successfully PULL one leg back while the other replaces it to the front it is now time for the important details and the actual B.S.step: Trenches. *

* Guidebook Note: If you're old enough to know the old 80's dance step "the Running Man" you've got it made! This step also includes the same non-weight PULL.

• **Trenches**

Now, to complete the traditional TRENCH, your PULL should travel in a semicircular motion (again off the outside of your toe as in the Over-the-Tops) around the side of your body as if you were a speed skater. You will swing both arms in opposition to your PULLING leg (in a windmill fashion) and keep all of your weight off of this PULL. *

PULL/STEP (as a one count action) X 4

(**1**234)

* Guidebook Note: TRENCHES were another Gene Kelly favorite; check out
Singin' in the Rain. Notice how he never looks up; hishead stays facing the
floor!

- **Shave and a Haircut**
  (The last two bars)
  JUMP/ "Double" PULLBACK(RIGHT)/STEP/BRUSH/
  HOP/SLAM *
  (12&a34 **12**3)

* Guidebook Note: "Shave and a haircut (BRUSH) two bits!" According to
Leonard Reed it's "ten cents . . ."

B.S. variations are endless . . .

Chapter Five
Vernacular Traditions – Oldies but Goodies

Tradition

Some Fun Traditions . . .

Here's a list of some of the traditional Vaudeville figures and steps that have had timeless appeal and deserve recognition but have not been featured in the previous chapters. All are variations of the guidebooks Basics, Rhythmic Words and Figures.

- **Shuffle Off To Buffalo (Basic)** — "The Buffalo"
  Frequently used as an exit step and continues to be popular with recital based dance organizations. *(See Reference Guide I - Terminology)*

  STEP/TRIPLE
  (1&a2)

- **Sugars (Sugar Foot)**
  A popular Swing Era move that takes STEPS in an exaggerated "turned-out" position to travel front twisting from one side of your body to the other. This action is usually shared with an equally exaggerated, shaking-hand action.

- **Shorty George**
  Another "swing" move that "turns in" the legs pigeon-toed and moves forward with hip and swaying knee action to the front. This move is usually accompanied by pointed fingers to the ground.

- **Boogie Woogie**
  This jazz basic jumps forward with two SINGLES and then

repeats moving back. Usually has a lifted kicking leg action prior to moving forward. This step likes to dance with Shorty George.

CLAP/STEP/STEP CLAP/STEP/STEP
(4a1) *forward* (2a3) *back*

- **Truckin'**
  A stylized SLIDE/HOP in the direction of the action leg that was usually executed with an index finger up, high and shakin'!

- **Scissors**
  Usually a combination of DOUBLE B/C's (BACK) crossing in the action of scissors turning pigeon-toed underneath the hips. Most common is a DOUBLE/SINGLE ESSENCE variation.

- **Bambalina**
  First action starts crossed with first SHUFFLE initiated over the supporting leg, the first TRIPLE open and the final TRIPLE crossed to the other side. This is actually a "Falling off the Log" variation that travels opposite of the first leg that creates sound.

  SHUFFLE/HOP/TRIPLE/TRIPLE
  (4&1&a2&3&)

- **Charleston**
  Repeats in the action of the popular dance craze from front to back with the TRIPLES and SHUFFLES executed to the sides.
  HOP/HOP/TRIPLE/SHUFFLE/HOP/SHUFFLE
  (12&a3&a4&a)

- **Falling Off The Log** (w/Heel Click)
  This figure crosses the non-weight-bearing leg in front of and behind to resemble balancing on a rolling log in water.

  HOP/TRIPLE/STEP/STEP/STEP/CLICK/HOP/CLICK/HOP

  (4&a12341a(2)a(3))

- **The Bill Bailey**
  Nowadays people know it as Michael Jackson's "Moonwalk" but the step was originally done by Mr. Bailey (Pearl Bailey's brother and a protege of Mr. Bill Robinson) way before Michael was born!

  * Guidebook Note: History is a wonderful thing. Take the time to find out who all of these artists were! *(See Appendix — Resources & Supplies.)*

- **Pigeon Toes**
  A traveling step that moves your legs in and out from "turned-in" or pigeon toed to "turned-out." This step is a great figure for adding HEEL and TOE work, thus creating two-footed CRAWLING CRAMP ROLLS.

  The Camel Walk, Barrel Turn, Coffee Grinders, Ballin' the Jack and Corkscrew are other movement foundations you can research within a jazz dance or musical theatre program among many others! *

* Guidebook Note: Check out many more of these traditional steps and where they came from in *Jazz Dance* **by Jean & Marshall Stearns and Mark Knowles'** *Tap Dance Dictionary (See Appendix).*

Your Continued Journey

It's Only the Beginning.

Soul

In Closing

I hope that you have been led to an endless world of rhythmic possibilities and a lifetime of tap creation through this guidebook! Whatever your level of expertise, it was my intent to have introduced to you a foundation of tap basics and a simple philosophy of movement that can be used as a beginner's tool and a springboard of choreography and improvisation for your **Soul** and your **Soles**.

I believe, as mentioned earlier, that simplicity and listening hold a basic truth. If you know your basics, practice (endlessly) for clarity and rhythm and listen to your world for creative ideas, you'll have it made!

May *The Souls of* **Your** *Feet* find their place in this wonderful world of tap dance and share your creations with many others.

Variations Reference
(See index for variation locations)

S/D/T/Q/Q

Rhythm Changes

Double-Up

Directions

Accent Changes

Toe Punch Add-Ons

Hop Variations

Home Base

Turn Variations

Combinations

Add-a-Heel

Graduate

Heel/Toe Replacements

Melody Change

Leap Variations

Continuations

Inserts

Tempo Change

Add-a-Drop

Polyrhythms

Travel

Silence Is Golden

Hop Variations

Rhythm Shifts

Mix & Match

Single/Double Time

Add-a-Hop

Start Variations

Slide Variations

Splits

Rhythmic Integrity

Backwards

Creation.

The Rhythm of Life

Appendix
Resources & Supplies

Tap

Shoes, Floors & Taps

Shoes

Most tap dancers nowadays are wearing an oxford style shoe of varying styles. Most of these dance shoes are available at your local retailer or by mail order at medium to high price ranges. Unfortunately, there is no such thing as an inexpensive tap shoe unless it's second hand or creatively designed from a comfortable pair of loafers or wingtips!

The most expensive is not necessarily the best. Each individual will have their own opinion as to which shoe works best for them as well as what taps to use and how tight to keep them. Again, all of us are unique and preferences will vary. Some dancers prefer a light shoe while others prefer some weight; some dancers prefer their shoes with double (instead of single) soles and every dancer is different when it comes to the fit. My preference is a heavier shoe with a double sole and the fit of a nice pair of walking shoes: *Dansky's (see Leo's for the new Bufalino shoe!)* with *Capezio Teletone* taps — a total price of about $175.00 after the taps are professionally "installed."

Here is a list of the most common tap shoe suppliers:

Capezio

Offers numerous varieties for children as well as adults to include shoes designed by Gregory Hines and Ira Bernstein. The professional choices are the *Gregory Hines, the K360* and the *Tone-Master.* This company also offers a Jazz-Tap shoe for flexible movement as well as heeled character shoes for women. Most high-end priced shoes will come without the taps, which will have to be purchased separately and attached by a shoe repair specialist.

Available from your local dancewear retailer, or call Capezio's NYC office at (212) 245-2150.

Dansky

This company offers a shoe originally designed by Brenda Bufalino and Avi Miller. This is my personal favorite; however, they conform better to a narrow or average-width foot. Brenda now has a shoe distributed by Leo called the *Bufalino! (see below).*

> ATDO, NYC. (U.S. Distributor)
> The Jazz Tap Center, Israel.
> *(See Organizations and Companies.)*

Leo's Dancewear, Inc.

This company also offers a variety of tap shoes including the *Split Sole Jazz Tap, The Alexander Concerto* designed by Lane Alexander and the soon to be released *Bufalino* designed by Brenda Bufalino.

Available from your local dancewear retailer. Find your local store by calling (773) 889-7700.

Revolution Dancewear

This company supplies "the most flexible tap shoe on the market" according to the Tap Dance Homepage.

> *Revolution Dancewear 1-800-806-1157*
> *www. revolutiondance.com*

For additional shoe information: Tap Dance Homepage *(see Sources of Tap Information).*

Taps

- *Capezio Teletone* taps — uses screws to attach to a supplied "soundboard".
- *Master* toe tap and *Duo-Tone* heel taps — use nails with no soundboard.
- *Morgan Toe* — uses screws.
- *Teletone #2* with the *Rayow System* — currently only available on the Capezio CG09. This "Gold Premier" shoe's toe tap has a single, adjustable screw for tone changes.

Floors

If you're searching for a dance studio, locate one with a sprung, wooden floor. Meaning a floor that is lifted and "sprung" off of the concrete foundation underneath. This will save you much time in the "ice department" nursing your shin splints. If the tap instructor is not sure what kind of floor they're teaching on, I would also try another location.

Unfortunately, it is sometimes unavoidable for those of us who perform to get a subpar floor. In fact, many contracts are signed by presenters that demand the supply of a "raised, wooden floor" only to find out that the theatre thinks we're talking about how far the stage is "raised" from the audience! It's often too late when you find out.

Raised, sprung floors not only safeguard you from undue injury but the tone qualities produced are clearly defined. A floor, which is directly on a concrete slab, produces a high-pitched single tone result whether the dancer is using the heels or the toes. The result could be compared to a trumpet with one note!

Portable Floors & Dance Mats

Portable dance mats are available from many sources most of which supply a 4x4 or 4x8 version. These floors consist of oak or maple sections backed by canvas which enables the floor to roll up for easy transport. Information on portable dance mats can be found by contacting:

Rusty Frank (818) 753-7968
RustyFrank@compuserve.com

The American Tap Dance Orchestra
(*See Tap Organizations and Companies.*)

Sources of Tap Information

The following reference guides and listings are compiled from my personal library as well as information from the International Tap Association and the Tap Dance Homepage. *(See listings below.)*

International Tap Association

c/o The Colorado Dance Festival

P.O. Box 356, Boulder, CO 80306

(303) 443-7989

www.tapdance.org/tap/

Tap's original networking machine of tap performance and workshop schedules, history, happenings and articles!

Dancer

Melba Huber (Tap Dance Writer)

2809 Bird Avenue, Suite 231

Miami, FL 33133

www.danceronline.com

Historian and tap ambassador Melba Huber writes a regular column on the tap dancers in the business past and present.

Tap Dance Homepage

www.tapdance.org

An online source of International Tap Association information and more! The best reference pages of videos and tap supplies around. Check out the film listings available on videotape for tap classics including Fred Astaire & Ginger Rogers, the Nicholas Brothers, John Bubbles, the Condos Brothers, Ruby Keeler and Bill Robinson!

Tap America Project

Carol Vaughn, Executive Director
P.O. Box 18505
Washington, DC 20036
(301) 589-6123
FAX (301) 585-4095
A Washington D.C. based nonprofit organization dedicated to the survival, preservation and future of tap dance!

Internet Search

A search for "tap dance" on the World Wide Web will bring all kinds of additional rhythm sites to your finger tips!

Kahnotation ©

This wonderful written method is a strong written foundation of tap technique and your creations. The most current reference found is Kahnotation: Computerized Notation for Tap Dance. In: *Dance Technology: Current Applications and Future Trends*, pp. 59- 63. National Dance Association.

Recommended Books

Tap! - The Greatest Tap Dance Stars & Their Stories
By Rusty Frank
A beautiful collection of interviews and biographical information on tap dancers from 1900-1955.

Jazz Dance
By Jean & Marshall Stearns
An excellent source of historical information on tap dance in its heyday including dance notation for most traditional jazz steps!

Inside Tap - Technique and Improvisation for Today's Tap Dancer
By Anita Feldman
This is a wonderful source of tap information from one of the most inventive tap choreographers today. This book covers not only Anita's personal style and teaching philosophy but is also a wonderful source of historical information. Really fun if you're into musical notation and rhythm games!

Footprints - A Tap Dancer's World
By Peter Petronio
This is an exquisite collection of the black and white photography of Mr. Peter Petronio. A wonderful collection of moments with tap dancer's and their musicians in performance and rehearsal.

Peter Petronio
45 Rue Chauvelot
92240 Malakoff   FRANCE

Tap Along With Tommy
By Tommy Sutton
I know, this sounds pretty hokey, but it is actually a nice collection of historical steps and dance philosophies from a career professional. It's quite a large collection and if you like deciphering combinations from books, this is for you! *

Weslock Enterprises
3189 Weslock Circle
Decatur, GA 30034
(404) 243-7196
Frost3189@aol.com
www.tapalong.com

* **Guidebook Note: True tap dance happens when you gain knowledge of the sounds and structures of history and music. Utilize written material to expand** *your* **creation options or to "get a feel" for another's voice. Spend more time on** *your* **feet exploring** *your* **voice!**

The Tap Dance Dictionary
By Mark Knowles
A 1998 release of definitions relating to tap dance. A dense collection of tap semantics and regionalisms for the left brain and a great collection of historical references. Not all definitions are included but 99.9% of them are! If you know what you're looking for and you have a foundation in the dance form this is a great resource!

Tap Roots - The Early History of Tap Dancing
By Mark Knowles
A 2000 release of an incredible history of tap dance that covers the influence of entire world cultures!

Tapworks
By Beverly Fletcher

A good solid reference manual for tap dance teachers from a respected professional dance educator. Tap history, terminology, styles and teaching levels set a strong foundation for curriculum and choroegraphy reference.

Brotherhood In Rhythm
By Constance Valis Hill

A beautifully written tribute to our beloved Nicholas Brothers.

Class Act - The Jazz Life of Choreographer Cholly Atkins
By Cholly Atkins & Jacqui Malone

A personal look into the life and legacy of our great dancing master Mr. Cholly Atkins.

Savion - My Life In Tap
By Savion Glover & Bruce Weber

Hittin', listenin', drummin' and hoofin' from Savion's incredible perspective.

Steppin' on the Blues
By Jacqui Malone

A 1996 release celebrating the history of African American vernacular dance and its accompanying meanings.

Video References

The best source of video and film listings around is on the Tap Dance Homepage *(see Sources of Tap Information)*. Some of my video favorites are listed below. (For classic films also locate the Tap Dance Homepage on the internet or the International Tap Association — *See Sources of Tap Information.)*

(★ not available commercially)

- **The Magic of "Honi" Coles** – A PBS presentation of this wonderful "class act" gentleman and his art. Produced by Susan Pollard. Get your local public station to present this loving tribute in your area! ★

- **Tap – Dance in America** – A PBS presentation hosted by Gregory Hines. Some of the best in the business in the late 1980's featuring Brenda Bufalino and the American Tap Dance Orchestra, a young Savion Glover, Tommy Tune, Fred Strickler, Camden Richman, Dianne Walker and more! ★

- **Songs Unwritten: A Tap Dancer Remembered** – A documentary on the wonderful Mr. Leon Collins and his melodic style.

The Leon Collins Archive Inc.
P.O. Box 28128
Philadelphia, PA 19131

- **By Word of Foot** – Archival footage of Jane Goldberg's 1980 Changing Times Tap Festival with rare footage of John Bubbles, "Honi" Coles, Gregory Hines and more!

  American Tap Dance Orchestra
  West Village Station
  P.O. Box 20212
  New York, NY 10014
  (212) 243-6438

- **Two Takes on Tap** – A wonderful video of two of the most influential female tap dancers in the world today, Brenda Bufalino (the American Tap Dance Orchestra) and Lynn Dally (the Jazz Tap Ensemble).

  American Tap Dance Orchestra

- **Great Feats of Feet** – A major collector's item produced by Brenda Bufalino featuring The Copasetics on a personal as well as professional level.

  American Tap Dance Orchestra

- **No Maps on My Taps** – Featuring the late Chuck Green, Bunny Briggs and Sandman Sims, this film offers a unique "backstage" look at these tap dance legends.

  Direct Cinema Ltd.
  P.O. Box 69799
  Los Angeles, CA 90069

- **About Tap** – A short and fairly dated video but one of the few archival tapes available of Mr. Jimmy Slyde, Steve Condos and Chuck Green.

  Direct Cinema
  P.O. Box 69799
  Los Angeles, CA 90069

- **We Sing, We Dance: The Nicholas Brothers** – Unfortunately another PBS documentary not available, but an incredible reference that airs often on numerous affiliate stations. ★

- **Instructional Videos from Brenda Bufalino**
  Vernacular Movement and the Time Step with Variations, B.S. Chorus/Old Soft Shoe Chorus, Improvisation and Afro-Cuban to Bop, Where the Action Is! and Double Time Series.

  American Tap Dance Orchestra
  West Village Station
  P.O. Box 20212
  New York, NY 10014

- **Tap Dancin'** – The pioneers and the young performers of the 1980's share the tap dance experience.

  Blackwood Films
  251 West 57th St.
  NYC, NY 10019

- **Leonard Reed's Shim Sham Shimmy** – A wonderfully produced video by Rusty Frank that features Mr. Reed himself!

  Rusty E. Frank

  (818) 753-7968 — RustyFrank@compuserve.com

- **The Essentials of Tap Technique** – A short piece featuring Brenda Bufalino, Charles "Cookie" Cook, Kevin Ramsey and "The B.S. Chorus"!

  Susan Goldbetter/Circuit Productions
  635 Caroll Street
  Brooklyn, NY 11215
  (718) 638-4878

- **Steve Condos' Workout /Double Digit Dancing** – The work of the late Steve Condos by the artist himself. A great source of information for you left-brainers out there looking for good tap dance "rudiments" and variations.

  Lorraine Condos, 317 W. 54th #2D, NYC 10019
  (212) 245-3352

- **Jazz Hoofer: The Legendary Baby Lawrence** – A wonderful archival collection of Mr. Lawrence and his wonderful be-bop style!

  Rhapsody Films, 30 Charlton St., NYC, NY 10014

- **The Dancing Man: Peg Leg Bates** – Another PBS documentary that is not available commercially. Set your VCR's!

Tap Dance Organizations and Companies

The American Tap Dance Orchestra (ATDO)
The International Tap Dance Orchestra
Founded and directed by Brenda Bufalino.
Professional performances specializing or orchestrated tap and polyrhythmic choreography. ATDO also handles numerous tap dance supplies.

West Village Station
P.O. Box 20212
NYC, NY 10014
(212) 243-6438

Tap City / The New York City Tap Festival
Tony Waag, Producer/Director
The Big Apple's international celebration of rhythm!

33 Little West 12th St.
NYC, NY 10014
(646)230-9564
www.nyctapfestival.com

The Jazz Tap Ensemble
Lynn Dally, Artistic Director
One of the oldest contemporary, concert tap dance companies specializing in jazz & contemporary tap improvisation and choreography.

(310) 475-4412/FAX (310) 475-4037

Manhattan Tap
Heather Cornell, Artistic Director
New York-based tap company working with solo artists and established masters in the field.

(212) 787-7181 phone/FAX

Rhapsody in Taps
Linda Sohl-Donnell, Artistic Director
Multiform ensemble utilizing tap as well as modern and other dance forms. Repertoire is extensive and includes contemporary as well as established master's works.

(213) 661-2172

Tapestry Dance Company & the Soul to Sole Festival
Acia Gray Executive/Artistic Director
Co-Founder, Deirdre Strand
Professional, nonprofit dance company specializing in the choreography and training of multi-discipline dance with a foundation in rhythm tap.

507 B Pressler
Austin, TX 78703
(512) 474-9846
dance@tapestry.org / www.tapestry.org

Chicago Human Rhythm Project
Lane Alexander, Director
Host of highly popular and diverse tap workshops, residencies and performances.

(773) 761-4889
CHRProject@aol.com

National Tap Ensemble

Chris Baker, Director

Markets twelve master dancers and musicians, with numerous educational programs and concerts.

P.O. Box 90187
Washington, D.C. 20090-0187
(301) 864-8277 or 1-888-NTE-TAPS
staff@usatap.org
www.usatap.org

Jazz Tap Center, New York / Tel Aviv

Avi Miller/Ofer Ben, Directors

P.O. Box 1050
New York, NY 10276

Avi@AviMiller.com

Fred Strickler & Friends - New Ideas on Tap

Fred Strickler, Director

Former member of the Jazz Tap Ensemble and current soloist and choreographer with Rhapsody in Taps.

fred.strickler@ucr.edu

Flying Foot Forum

Joe Chvala, Director

1820 Sevens Avenue South #10
Minneapolis, MN 55403
(612) 874-6664

Portsmouth Percussive Dance Festival
Drika Overton, Artstic Director

P.O. Box 4023
Portsmouth, NH 03802

ppdf@jazzandtap.com

Ten Toe Percussion
Ira Bernstein, Director
Collection of international percussive dance artists of all kinds including clog, Irish step dance and tap.

(828) 255-9393 — IraTenToe@aol.com

The Robert L. Reed Tap Heritage Institute, Inc.
Robert Reed, Director
St. Louis-based organization that hosts the St. Louis Tap Festival.

3148 Halliday Avenue
St. Louis, MO 63118-1208

Zapped Taps (tm)
Alfred Desio, Director
A division of The Los Angeles Choreographers & Dancers. Mr. Desio is the inventor of Tap-Tronics (tm).

Los Angeles Choreographers & Dancers
Louise Reichlin, Managing Director
louisehr@bcf.usc.edu

Feet 2 the Beat
Rod Ferrone, Max Pollak

(212) 749-5789 — hooferboy@aol.com

Tappers With Attitude
Renee Kreithen & Yvonne Edwards, Co-Directors
Youth group representing the greater Washington, DC area. Repertoire includes works of contemporary as well as established masters.

Knock on Wood Tap Studio
8700 Georgia Avenue
Silver Spring, Maryland 20910
(301) 495-0395

Hip Tap Project
Leela Petronio, Artistic Director

(33)-06-86-28-12-03

The Swift Brothers
George Hohagen, John Kloss

(708) 351-1597

San Francisco Tap Dance Center
Rosie Radiator, Director
Home of the Rad Tap Team

540 Alabama Street
San Francisco, CA 94110
(415) 621-TAPS or 1-800-RAD-TAPS

North Carolina Youth Tap Ensemble (NCYTE)
Gene Medler, Artistic Director

(919) 967-9624

Northeast Tap Connection

A nonprofit organization for tap dance enthusiasts formed to foster the communication in the Northeast U.S. tap community.

76 Beech Ridge Rd., Scarbrough, Maine 04074
ntcemail@aol.com

Anita Feldman Tap

Anita Feldman, Artistic Director

Well established company by *Inside Tap* author. Inventive choreography of modern and contemporary rhythm tap works.

(516) 944-6673

Rhythm in Shoes

Sharon Leahy, Founder/Choreographer

Ohio based company includes tap, step dancing and integrated numerous skits.

(937) 226-SHOE

Tap Team Two

Robert Burden/Arthur Leo Taylor

Perform and teach in the Philadelphia area.

(215) 546-2294

Southeastern Tap Explosion

Contact: Mitch Jablow

3641 Clubland Drive
Marietta, GA 30068
(770)971-2993

Recommended Master Teachers

This is a list of my personal favorite teachers that I feel have a strong foundation in the tap dance community and are excellent sources of additional information to extend your rhythmic voice! These artists are recommended from experiencing their teaching and/or choreographic techniques directly. This is in no way a complete reference guide for the teachers of tap dance who bless this world with their feet!

If you have a chance to work with any of these artists, I would highly recommend you take the opportunity! Many teach at numerous tap dance festivals and with tap dance communities throughout America and abroad. For scheduling information of most of these dancers their performances and teaching schedules, check out the **Tap Dance Homepage** or join the **International Tap Association**. *(See Sources of Tap Information.)* Both of these references have more complete information on dancers around the world. Remember that individual style is the beauty of this artform and all teachers offer unique rhythmic experiences.

Brenda Bufalino – A leading female pioneer of the form having directly influenced the beginning of concert tap dance. Ms. Bufalino is the Artistic Director of the American & International Tap Dance Orchestras. Greatly influenced by her past partner Charles "Honi" Coles, she definitely has her own incredible and unique musical style that has directly or indirectly influenced most professional tap dancers worldwide. Tap orchestrations and tone qualities are Ms. Bufalino's specialty.

Sarah Petronio – A true vocalist with her feet, this artist has been greatly influenced by her past (and sometimes present partner) Jimmy Slyde but sings from a strong be-bop elegance of her own. Always honest on stage and off with her presentation of rhythm, Ms. Petronio has much to share in this world of rhythm communication.

Dianne Walker – Elegance and a wonderful sense of humor personified. Ms. Walker is a living legacy of Mr. Leon Collins yet shares her own rhythmic life with style and grace.

Jan Feager – Former Artistic Director of St. Louis' *Tapsichore*, Ms. Feager graces the stage and her classes with a symphonic sensitivity.

Mark Mendonca – Mr. Mendonca is a strong percussive artist who loves riffs and speed and has the looks to sell 'em. Past member of the highly popular Steps Ahead Tap Trio as well as the Jazz Tap Ensemble among others.

Lane Alexander – Currently the director of the Chicago Human Rhythm Project, Mr. Alexander tours the world as soloist and master teacher performing works such as *Morton Gould's Tap Dance Concerto*. He's a past member of Austin On Tap and the National Tap Dance Company of Canada.

Bruce Stegmann – Former Artistic Director of Chicago's *Especially Tap Company*. Mr. Stegmann's style is diverse, fun and funky.

Henry LeTang – The master of Broadway and beyond. Responsible for numerous commissions to include *Sophisticated Ladies*, *The Wiz*, *Black & Blue* and the movies *Tap* and *The Cotton Club*. Fast paced and traditional, Mr. LeTang's classes are a major workout!

Gregory Hines – Tap dance's ambassador is usually too busy, but if you get a chance grab it!

Savion Glover – Tap dance's living future. Diverse, hard hitting and complex. He can do anything.

Leela Petronio – Definitely her mother's prodigy (Sarah Petronio) but taking the form to her own Hip Hop cutting edge.

Steve Zee – A class act as performer and teacher. Based in California, Mr. Zee's credits include *The Hot Shoe Shuffle,* the Jazz Tap Ensemble as well as into TV land as the magic behind the tap dancing Hershey's kisses.

Lynn Dally – Brings the concert dancer to rhythm tap through her company the Jazz Tap Ensemble. Ms. Dally is a forerunner in the early 1980's renaissance of tap.

Sam Weber – As principal dancer with the Jazz Tap Ensemble, Mr. Weber's style is impeccable and his relaxation technique is groundbreaking! A former Joffrey ballet dancer, he truly utilizes his full body to communicate his rhythms.

Katherine Kramer – A pioneer of "Tap Salons", Mr. Kramer is a wonderful master teacher as well as historian. Her career has spanned the last two decades with all the right connections.

Anita Feldman – A leading innovator in contemporary tap dance work as well as the inventor of the "Tap Dance Instrument." Author of *Inside Tap* and Artistic Director of Anita Feldman Tap.

Dr. Jimmy Slyde – As his name implies, he's the master of slides and he's the Duke of Elegance! His style is smooth, thoughtful, honest and playful. One of our last first generation masters around!

Dr. Cholly Atkins – The legs and brains behind the Motown movement! Mr. Atkins brought his tap career (with partner Charles "Honi" Coles) to Detroit and staged and directed countless vocal artists (including The Temptations and The Supremes!) between 1953-1994! If you look close, you'll see the Shim Sham Shimmy in those moves!

LaVaughn Robinson – A wonderful artist of speed and the Paddle and Roll. Often performs with the also wonderful Germaine Ingram.

Fred Strickler – A wonderfully sensitive and thoughtful musician as well as a pioneer of the tap renaissance.

The following individuals are also souls to be sought after for an incredible array of technique, history and style! This is only a personalized list based on my experiences. This is not intended to be a complete source listing . . .

Dr. Leonard Reed, Dr. Fayard Nicholas, Dr. Jeni LeGon, Dr. Bunny Briggs, Barbara Duffy, Josh Hilberman, Linda Sohl-Donnell, Heather Cornell, Ted Levy, Ayodele Casel, Max Pollack, Chris Baker, Tony Waag, Margaret Morrison, Germaine Ingram, Dormesia Sumbry-Edwards, Omar Edwards, Bob Carroll, Debra Bray, Fred Moritel, Rusty Frank, Jane Goldberg, Roxane Butterfly, Robert Reed, Nicole Hockenberry, Ira Bernstein, Deborah Mitchell, Gracey Tune, Christy Wyant, Barbara Phillips, Tobias Tak, Van Porter, Jay Fagan, Laurie Johnson, Debbie Dee, Bril Barrett and **Jeannie Hill.**

Index

Index